WITH GLORY AND HONOR YOU CROWNED THEM

THE FEMALE MARTYRS OF THE ROMAN CANON

MATTHEW MANINT

TAMANRASSET PRESS

2019

Tamanrasset Press
325 Hiller Dr.
Biloxi, MS 39531

First Edition 2019

ISBN 978-0-359-89235-8

10 9 8 7 6 5 4 3 2 1

Dedicated to my dearest Saint Cecilia

And all female martyrs, especially those known only to God

A special note of gratitude to Kate Essenberg, who humbled my original draft of this work with her indefatigable editing prowess. To help ease the sting, she drew little cartoons on the draft manuscript. I have included one below.

She is a gem.

This book is set in the typeface *Perpetua*, which was first used in 1929 for a translation of *The Passion of Perpetua and Felicity* by Walter H. Shewring.
Its creator was Eric Gill.

A full-color, high-resolution PDF of this book may be downloaded at no charge from coastcaritas.org.

CONTENTS

INTRODUCTION

Since we are watched from above by such a cloud of witnesses, let us rid ourselves of all that weighs us down, of the sinful habit that clings so closely, and run, with all endurance, the race for which we are entered.

Hebrews 12:1[1]

This book came about through the direct intercession of two saints—Cecilia and Agnes. In 2015, I joined about 45 young men and women on a pilgrimage through Italy for the 25th anniversary of the founding in Rome of the Apostoli della Vita Interiore—the Apostles of the Interior Life. In 2003, I was fortunate enough to spend five months in Rome discerning with the community. Although God called me elsewhere, I remained in close contact with the Apostles and was eager to meet them again for this celebration. Little did I know that Saints Cecilia and Agnes were also arranging their meetings with me.

As I read over the itinerary for the journey, St. Cecilia kept breaking into my thoughts. Our last destination would be Rome, where she was martyred and buried. I decided to dedicate my pilgrimage to her, and I asked friends and family to send me any prayers and intercessions they would like me to bring on the

[1] Unless otherwise indicated, all scriptural passages are from the Msgr. Ronald Knox translation.

The Virgin with Child. St. Cecilia, and St. Agnes

Francesco Vanni, **c.1600**

Museo del Prado, Madrid

pilgrimage. I entreated Cecilia to beg God's graces be poured out abundantly on myself, my fellow pilgrims, and all whose intercessions I carried with me on a sheet of paper that would be left at her tomb.

The pilgrimage was a graced time of fellowship and reflection, and I diligently carried the petitions to St. Cecilia's church and left them on the altar. My task completed, I decided to allow the Holy Spirit to guide my last unplanned days of solo pilgrimage in Rome. One day, wandering towards the Tiber River, I happened to enter St. Agnes's Church at Piazza Navona. The piazza was built upon on the site of the former Stadium of Domitian, which was used for such events as footraces and gladiatorial combats. It was a smaller stadium and seated perhaps 15,000 to 20,000 spectators. Some of the arcades around it were used as brothels, and it was to one of these that the young St. Agnes was condemned in the reign of Diocletian for being a Christian. When God miraculously halted any assault on Agnes's chastity, the exasperated Roman soldiers executed her by the sword.

I entered her church and went into a side chapel. There, I was stunned to see the small, delicate skull of a girl perhaps 12 years of age—St. Agnes. It rested in a rectangular silver reliquary. At the center was a wreath of green enamel that recalled the evergreen wreaths that were laid at the graves of virgin martyrs in the early Church. The wreath framed the glass-covered, circular portal through which her little skull could be seen.

The shrine and skull of St. Agnes, Rome[1]

[1] Images from Michaelphillipr (CC BY-SA 3.0).

It was a moment of such tenderness, intimacy, and beauty. Agnes's life and witness seemed to echo there with her mortal remains. This pure, brave girl, condemned by Rome to be murdered in obscurity before her life had even bloomed, was still alive, still known. Though she died over 1,700 years ago, she was radiantly present in the Body of Christ, and there did not seem to be any barrier of time or death to separate us. In the presence of this "dead bone," there was a torrent of life that would never fade into a forgotten past.

Seeing this ancient skull of a mere child who gave her life because of her faith, I meditated on the contrast of Agnes and the Empire that murdered her in the days that followed. When I was speaking to the pilgrims at the Forum, I said, "Only the ruins of the Roman Empire remain. And yet, look at what is still alive and here today—the Church and the witness of the saints. This mighty empire, like all others, did not last. But Christ remains."

These memorable encounters sowed the seed of the desire to know more about not only Saints Agnes and Cecilia, but the other 5 female martyrs that are memorialized in the Roman Canon—that most august of Eucharistic Prayers in the Catholic Mass. For centuries, their names have been intoned throughout the world in every Mass, and yet their stories are little known.

The saints, even those who perished over a millennia ago, have a freshness, a newness that transcends the dust of the years to inspire us to imitation. It is this newness that I experienced in the ability of St. Agnes to transfix my heart and speak across the centuries, saying, "You can do this! I will pray for you and walk with you for the rest of your pilgrimage." May St. Agnes and her six companions lead all of us to run the race of sanctity with faith and boldness.

THE ROMAN CANON

The Roman Canon is the portion of the Mass that contains the pinnacle of the entire liturgy—the consecration of the bread and wine into the glorified body of Jesus Christ.[1] From the beginning, Christians have celebrated the Mass in obedience to Christ's admonition at the Last Supper to offer a perpetual sacrifice in remembrance of Him.[2] The references to this memorial service in both the New Testament and other early documents highlight the act of a solemn blessing of the bread and wine, and warn those in the Church to not receive the Eucharist in a state of sin. The Church treated the consecrated elements with particular care and reverence, and ensured that the least particle of it not be lost or profaned.

It is not within the scope of this brief chapter to elaborate and defend the proposition that the early Church viewed the Mass as a sacrificial, not merely symbolic, action. Taking this sacrificial view for granted, then, it makes sense that the Church would especially treasure the Canon: the part of the Mass that is, essentially, one long Eucharistic prayer in which the sacrificial consecration resides.

[1] "This food we call the Eucharist, of which no one is allowed to partake except one who believes that the things we teach are true, and has received the washing for forgiveness of sins and for rebirth, and who lives as Christ handed down to us. For we do not receive these things as common bread or common drink; but as Jesus Christ our Savior being incarnate by God's Word took flesh and blood for our salvation, so also we have been taught that the food consecrated by the Word of prayer which comes from him, from which our flesh and blood are nourished by transformation, is the flesh and blood of that incarnate Jesus."—St. Justin Martyr, *First Apology*, c.150. A.D. http://www.newadvent.org/fathers/0126.htm

[2] Luke 22:19.

The Elevation of the Host (from a Missal used at Mass)

Master of the Brussels Initials, c. 1395

The J. Paul Getty Museum, Los Angeles

Greek, the common language of Christians outside Palestine, was the language of the earliest Masses. The different centers of Catholicism, such as Antioch, Alexandria, and Rome, formed their own rites of the Mass that still share the main foundational elements. In the third and fourth centuries, Latin gained dominance in the West. St. Pope Gregory I standardized the Latin Roman Canon in the 7th century, and it has remained unchanged to this day. Before the radical liturgical changes that occurred after the Second Vatican Council (1962-1965), the Roman Canon was the Eucharistic prayer used at every Latin Rite Mass. After the 1960s, it is one of four.

Framing the words of consecration in the Canon ("This is my body.... This is my blood....") are two lists of saints and martyrs. The priest "celebrates their memory, as though to invite them, as 'kings and priests' (Apoc. 5:10), to offer the Sacrifice along with us, and by their powerful intercession and abundant merits to support our weak prayers, so that by the strength of their mediation we may experience God's help and protection in all situations and necessities." [1] Those named before the words of consecration include the blessed Virgin Mary, 12 Apostles, and 12 martyrs. After the consecration, the priest implores the intercession of 15 saints, including our seven female martyrs:

> *To us, also, your servants, who, though sinners, hope in your abundant mercies, graciously grant some share and fellowship with your holy Apostles and Martyrs: with John the Baptist, Stephen, Matthias, Barnabas, Ignatius, Alexander, Marcellinus, Peter,* ***Felicity, Perpetua, Agatha, Lucy, Agnes, Cecilia, Anastasia*** *and all your Saints; admit us, we beseech you, into their company, not weighing our merits, but granting us your pardon, through Christ our Lord.*

[1] Gehr, Nickolaus, *The Holy Sacrifice of the Mass: Dogmatically, Liturgically, and Ascetically Explained* (St. Louis: B. Herder, 1902), 607.

Fresco in the Catacomb of Callixtus, Rome, early 200s
This Christian fresco uses the common symbolism of an offering of fish upon a table to depict the Eucharist. Early Christians often visited the catacombs to offer the Mass, especially near the resting places of martyrs.

In most modern Catholic parishes, priests rarely pray the Roman Canon at Mass, normally preferring the shorter second or third Eucharistic Prayers. As liturgical scholar Enrico Mazza stated, "its use today is so minimal as to be statistically irrelevant." [2] Thus, today the names of our seven martyrs that were honored through the centuries in countless Masses are seldom heard. May this little book, in which their lives are presented in the same order that they are listed in the Canon,

[2] Mazza, Enrico, *The Eucharistic Prayers of the Roman Rite* (New York: Pueblo Publishing Company, 1986), xxxi.

be my contribution to keeping their stories alive so that all in need of their prayers might find seven dear friends close at hand.

FELICITY AND PERPETUA

Martyred *on March 7, 203* A.D. *in the Roman Amphitheater, Carthage*

Feast Day—*March 7th*

This anniversary feast calls to mind, in a manner fresh and new, that day whereon those blessed servants of God, Perpetua and Felicity, being nobly adorned with the crowns of martyrdom, did achieve the flower of perpetual felicity. They bore in the battle the name of Christ, and in the prize of battle found their own.

St. Augustine, *On the Birthday of the Martyrs Perpetua and Felicity*

The Roman Empire, notorious for its extravagant and creative methods of torture and execution, did have a few standards of decency. For one, it would not execute a pregnant woman. This scruple explained why the young slave Felicity, perhaps 20 years old, was still sitting in prison in Carthage, North Africa. After she gave birth, she would die in the arena.

Like most civilizations, Rome understood the power that came from public executions. The deaths of those whom the state considered dangerous served several functions. For one, all could see that the government brooked no patience for lawbreakers, and there was no mercy or wavering in its punishments. There may also have been a deterrent effect from seeing a criminal pulled to pieces in the arena.

However, the sinister genius of the Romans was to tap into the primal lust for violence and justice and turn it into a sophisticated show. As the development of these entertainments progressed, executions joined a panoply of other demonstrations, such as gladiator combats, fighting animals, and recreations of famous battles. At times, these events would last for days, and not only drew crowds of pagans, but Jews and Christians, as well.

Rome was a civilization that strictly divided citizens and non-citizens. The state gave Roman citizens certain protections and benefits, especially when it came to criminal punishment. Citizens sentenced to death were usually beheaded with some amount of dignity. Therefore, it often fell on those outside the citizen class, such as slaves and prisoners of war, to bear the more bizarre punishments of the arena. However, as seen in the case of Perpetua and her companions, even Roman citizens could be horrifically dispatched in the stadium if the local administrator deemed it a necessary exception to set an example.

The wide variety of torments arguably sprang from a few sources. The annals of history show that humanity craves the spectacle of violence, and also has a knack for coming up with ever more brutal ways to watch others suffer. As the centuries wore on, spectators in the arena not only saw beheadings, burnings, and male gladiatorial combats; in later years, dwarfs and obese women fought each other to the death, nude female gladiators made an appearance, and even Commodus the Emperor clubbed injured citizens while pretending he was Hercules fighting the Giants of Phanagoria.[1] So, the sadistic escalation may have been the result of a civilization that was glutting

[1] Kyle, Donald, *Spectacles of Death in Ancient Rome* (London: Routledge, 2001) 224-225.

itself on public violence but could not be sated without ever more intense experiences.

Another reason came from the aforementioned division between citizens and all others. Noncitizens needed to be continually reminded of their inferiority, and citizens required assurance that the State would protect their estimable status. Therefore, the punishments of noncitizens took on a bestial nature to demonstrate that they were little better than animals. For example, in 167 B.C. some noncitizens from foreign lands deserted from the Roman army. They were stomped to death by elephants in the arena, and the impact was so powerful that the Romans made this killing by animals (*damnatio ad bestias*) a regular part of nearly every arena show. People were dragged to death by animals, disemboweled by animals, and even raped by animals, all to the excited gasps and cheers of the crowd.[2]

This was the reality that faced Felicity, Perpetua, and their companions in the spring of 203 A.D. Even though their deaths on the Nones of March occurred a mere 170 years after Jesus Christ's Passion, we know a remarkable amount about what they endured, largely because Perpetua wrote an account. This narrative (part of a more extensive work called a *Passio*, or "Passion") is the earliest surviving example of its kind and is deemed authentic by nearly all modern scholars. Using this *Passio* narrative, based on a translation by R.E.

[2] According to the ancient Roman poet Martial in his *On the Public Shows of Domitian*, the Romans would recreate in the arena scenes from mythology, such as Pasiphae's coupling with a bull: "Believe that Pasiphae was enamoured of a Cretan bull: we have seen it. The old story has been confirmed. Let not venerable antiquity boast itself, Caesar; whatever fame celebrates, thy arena reproduces for thee." http://www.tertullian.org/fathers/martial_on_the_games_of_domitian_01_text.htm

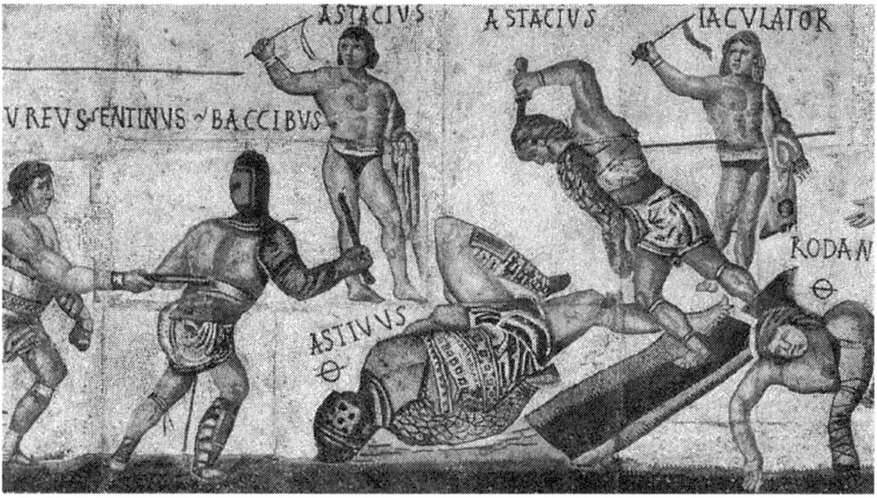

Gladiator mosaic in the Galleria Borghese, Rome, early 300s A.D. This work depicts different types of gladiators and weapons, along with the names of each combatant. The Greek symbol *theta* (θ) likely refers to θάνατος (death), and indicates the dead gladiators.

***Venator* (hunter) mosaic, Galleria Borghese, Rome, early 300s A.D.**

Wallis from the 19th century, let us go back to ancient North Africa and see how these saints lived and died.[3]

On a hill about 30 miles from the Mediterranean coast, 15 miles from ancient Carthage (the modern Tunisian city of Tunis), stands the ruins of Thuburbo Minus: the town that Perpetua, Felicity, Revocatus, Saturus, Saturninus, and Secundulus called home. This region of North Africa was a melting pot of tribes and religions that was the bane of Rome hundreds of years prior when Hannibal threatened the Empire from his capital of Carthage. From 149-146 B.C., Rome threw her entire weight behind the Third Punic War to, once and for all, bring Carthage to heel. In the Roman Senate, the famous orator Cato the Elder would end every speech with "*Carthago delenda est*"—"Carthage must be destroyed." Ultimately, the general Scipio Aemilianus and his legions razed Carthage to the ground in 146 B.C., and turned Africa (which the Romans named after a Berber tribe) into a Roman territory. The infamous Carthaginian stubbornness and power, far from being extinguished by Rome, would find new expression in the resistance of North African Christians to the Roman State. Some, such as Perpetua and her companions, would turn the arena to their advantage by using it as a platform for spreading the message of Christianity that would eventually convert the Empire.

The teachings of Christianity likely came to Carthage from Rome and from the Jews who were able to flee the destruction of Jerusalem in 70 A.D. by the Legions of Titus. In the beginning, Christianity was an esoteric offshoot of Judaism, so its teachings and followers were tucked within Jewish communities throughout the Empire. As Christianity spread, it brought more Gentiles under its sway. When it reached Carthage, it successfully converted people whose Phoenician

[3] Wallis, R.E., *The Passion of the Holy Martyrs Perpetua and Felicity*. From *Ante-Nicene Fathers*, Vol. 3. Edited by Alexander Roberts, James Donaldson, and A. Cleveland Coxe. (Buffalo, NY: Christian Literature Publishing Co., 1885.)

religious heritage included acts of child sacrifice. Gradually, more Gentile families of varying social classes converted to the new faith and formed a kind of underground community, always on the watch for the changing winds of persecution.

However, in the beginning, Perpetua, Felicity, and three of their companions—Revocatus, Secundulus, and Saturninus—were simple catechumens (from the Greek *katechoumenos* in Galatians 6:6), meaning that they were in the process of becoming Christians and were unbaptized. Saturus was their Catechism instructor, responsible for teaching them the Faith. In the early Church, it often took several years to become a member. Prospective converts were gradually taught the Faith until they were deemed ready to receive the sacraments of Baptism, Confirmation, and the Eucharist. This formation was not only to ensure that converts were morally and intellectually able to hold fast to their faith in the midst of a pagan culture, but also that they might be ready to endure periods of persecution.

Vibia Perpetua was a married noblewoman whose family, the Vibii, were a military family of distinction. Saturus, Saturninus, and Secundulus were freemen, and Felicity and Revocatus were slaves. Slavery was an essential part of Roman society, and the Empire had come to rely on the free labor for its financial advantage. Its abolition was not yet a critical issue for the Faith; St. Paul even sent the runaway slave Onesimus back to his master Philemon, along with a letter of explanation that became part of the New Testament. Felicity was most likely Perpetua's slave, perhaps coming from a family whose tribe attempted to rebel against Rome, as failed rebellions were an abundant source of slaves.[4] However, within the Church, there was no distinction between slaves and freemen. All five attended the first part

[4] Farina, William, *Perpetua of Carthage, Portrait of a Third-Century Martyr* (London: McFarland & Company, Inc., 2009), 191.

of the Mass[5] and Saturus's classes; all five desired the same goal of sanctity. All five, with Saturus, would be imprisoned and executed together by the State.

Soon after their deaths, an anonymous author took up Perpetua's narrative of the events (along with a brief vision written by Saturus) and added a preface and conclusion. The preface proposed that, just as ancient texts were written about the wonders of faith so that "God may be honored, as man may be strengthened", so too would this work set forth a "modern", marvelous tale of martyrdom for posterity, that no one would "suppose that the divine grace abode only among the ancients."

The unknown author may have met the martyrs, for he referred to their story as something "we have heard and handled," an allusion to the very first verse of the first letter of St. John. There, St. John declared that his readers might trust his proclamations about Jesus, for The Word is "what we have heard...what it was that met our gaze, and the touch of our hands." Going on, the author again echoed St. John by stating that he was writing this story down so that its readers "may have communion with the blessed martyrs, and through them with the Lord Jesus Christ," just as John wrote his letter so that "you too may share in our fellowship. Fellowship with the Father, and with his Son Jesus Christ." [6]

[5] In the early Church of both East and West, catechumens could not stay for the latter half of the Mass that included the prayer of Consecration and distribution of communion. The first part of the Mass that they were allowed to attend was called the "Mass of Catechumens".
[6] 1 John 1:3.

THE STRUGGLE BEGINS

Perpetua's historical account began after the arrest of the five catechumens. Saturus also turned himself in so that he might encourage and suffer with his students. Perpetua, described as a 22-year-old noblewoman with an "infant at the breast," received a visit from her pagan father. She lamented that he could not understand why she was obstinately clinging to her beliefs. The following dialog, along with all subsequent dialog and quotations from the *Passio*, are adapted from the aforementioned translation by R.E. Wallis:

> *"Father, do you see, let us say, this vessel lying here to be a little pitcher?"*
>
> *"I see it to be so."*
>
> *"Can it be called any other name than what it is?"*
>
> *"No."*
>
> *"Neither can I call myself anything else than what I am, a Christian."*
>
> *Then my father, provoked at this saying, threw himself upon me, as if he would tear my eyes out. But he only distressed me, and went away overcome by the devil's arguments.*

Perpetua's humanity shines through her words because she recorded her emotional life. Her sanctity did not nullify or destroy her sensitive nature but helped her master her feelings so that she could do what was necessary. She related that she was inspired at her baptism to ask for the grace of endurance for the trials to come, for a few days later the prisoners were moved and their suffering began:

> *"We are taken into the dungeon, and I was very much afraid, because I had never felt such darkness. O terrible day! O the fierce heat of the shock of the soldiery, because of the crowds! I was very unusually distressed by my anxiety for my infant."*

The Alexamenos Graffito, Palatine Hill Museum, Rome, c. 200
The earliest known depiction of Jesus Christ is a blasphemous graffito making fun of "Alexamenos worshiping his god." The donkey head was considered an insult in Roman society. The traced drawing is from *Ancient Rome in the Light of Recent Discoveries* by Rodolfo Lanciani, 1898.

Two deacons, Tertius and Pomponius, bribed the soldiers to allow the prisoners to be brought out of the miserable dungeon into a better part of the prison for a few hours, and Perpetua was finally able to feed her son. She obtained permission to bring him into the dungeon with her, and was so overjoyed at his presence that "the dungeon became to me as it were a palace, so that I preferred being there to being elsewhere." While meeting with her mother and one of her brothers (who was also a catechumen), her brother encouraged her to ask God for a vision that will reveal what was to come. "Tomorrow, I will tell you," she boldly replied.

THE VISION OF THE LADDER

In her vision, Perpetua saw a golden ladder that soared into the heavens. It was very narrow, and was covered with every kind of sword, lance, blade, and hook, such that anyone who was careless or inattentive would be cut to pieces. At the base of the ladder lurked an enormous dragon who sought to attack and frighten all who attempted to climb. She watched her teacher, Saturus, begin his ascent. He successfully reached the top, turned, held out his hand, and cried, "Perpetua, I am waiting for you! Be careful that the dragon does not bite you!" Nerving herself, Perpetua boldly declared, "In the name of the Lord Jesus Christ he shall not hurt me!" As the dragon prowled closer to her, she stepped forward and planted her foot upon the beast's head.

Nearing the top of the ladder, she saw a verdant garden filled with thousands of people in white robes. She noticed a towering man with white hair who wore a shepherd's garb and was milking sheep. He turned his gentle gaze to her and said, "You are welcome here, daughter." He handed her a small cake made with sheep's milk. She received the little cake and ate it as the thousands around said, "Amen."

Saint Perpetua with the Vision of the Heavenly Ladder

Jacques Callot, 17th century

Harvard Art Museums/Fogg Museum

Perpetua then awoke from her dream with an incredible sweetness lingering in her mouth. She then understood that her trial will end in martyrdom.

At this point, it would be appropriate to investigate the symbolism of Perpetua's dream. The ladder that stretches to the heavens is a classic metaphor of the spiritual life that hearkens back all the way to the book of Genesis, where Jacob saw a ladder upon which angels ascended and descended from Heaven to earth.[7] The early Church Fathers used the image of a ladder to Heaven as a means of explaining the ascetic struggle required to move away from an earthly life of sin and vice to the heights of sanctity. The Ladder of Divine Ascent, written by St. John Cassian in the 5th century, views the ladder as a kind of vertical understanding of Jesus's warning, "How narrow the road that leads on to life, and how few there are that find it!" [8] In a classic icon based off of Cassian's work, coal-black demons trip and pull at the climbers, angels and men watch the struggle, and Christ waits at the top with open arms. At the bottom a massive gray head balefully swallows one of the fallen.

As Perpetua's dream illustrates, only those who place their trust in Jesus Christ and successfully navigate the narrow path of the ladder with His grace can make it to the top and trample the beast underfoot. When she reached the top, she saw a vision of paradise, where Christ the Good Shepherd tends His sheep amidst thousands of saints in white. Her eating of the cake is an explicit reference to the Eucharist, for it is a foretaste and promise of Heaven whose sweetness lingered beyond her dream. Upon waking, she received an intuition that martyrdom

[7] Genesis 28:10-17.
[8] Matthew 7:14.

The Ladder of Divine Ascent

Late 12th century

St. Catherine's Monastery, Mt. Sinai

awaits— "I immediately related this to my brother, and we understood that it was to be a passion, and we ceased henceforth to have any hope in this world."

THE TRIAL

Shortly after, Perpetua's father visited her again and begged, "Lay aside your courage." He implored her not to deliver up her family to the scorn of men, and to consider the fate of her little boy. When the prisoners were led to the public forum to be interrogated and tried, her father met them there, and even brought the infant with him to sway her resolve. The procurator Hilarianus saw this pathetic situation and pleaded with Perpetua in a dialogue that pierces the centuries:

> *"Spare the grey hairs of your father, spare the infancy of your boy; offer sacrifice for the well-being of the emperors."*
>
> *"I will not do so."*
>
> *"Are you a Christian?"*
>
> *"I am a Christian."*
>
> *And as my father stood there to cast me down from the faith, he was ordered by Hilarianus to be thrown down, and was beaten with rods. And my father's misfortune grieved me as if I myself had been beaten, I so grieved for his wretched old age. The procurator then delivered judgment on all of us, and condemned us to the wild beasts, and we went down cheerfully to the dungeon.*

It is not clear from the text why Hilarianus ordered the beating of Perpetua's father, but it may have been due to his having knowledge of her conversion, or for having produced a daughter who had such contempt for the Roman reverence for family and state. Not only did she refuse to sacrifice to the emperor who was the guiding father of the Empire, but she defied her own father's authority and refused to put her child's welfare above her beliefs.[9] Besides, Christianity views all other gods as false, calling into question the legitimacy of the panoply of gods upon whom Rome relied for her welfare. Thus, Perpetua and her companions were enemies of the state; her father, due to the actions of his daughter, was therefore a failure.

After his humiliation in front of the crowd, her father refused to allow Perpetua's son to stay with her in the dungeon. The text does not mention whether she saw her child again.

THE VISIONS OF DINOCRATES

During a time when the prisoners were praying together, Perpetua received an inspired word—*Dinocrates*. It was the name of her deceased brother, who was only seven years old when he died of cancer. She began to pray intensely for him. That night, she received a vision of Dinocrates wandering out from a gloomy place. He was gasping with thirst, covered in dirt and grime, and his face still bore the ghastly wound where the cancer worked freely, a wound that "caused repugnance to all men." He stumbled towards a large basin filled with water, but it was too high for him to reach. Perpetua grieved that there was a chasm separating her from her tormented brother, and she could not cross to help him. It called to her mind the chasm that separated the thirsting, tormented rich man from the paradise that held Lazarus:[10]

> *"I trusted that my prayer would bring help to his suffering; and I prayed for him every day until we passed over into the prison of the camp, for we were to fight in the camp-show. Then was the birthday of*

[9] Farina, 50.
[10] Luke 16:26

> *Geta Caesar,*[11] *and I made my prayer for my brother day and night, groaning and weeping that he might be granted to me."*

The importance of this segment of the text cannot be overstated, for it demonstrates a belief in the early Christian community that prayer was efficacious for those who had died. Though Perpetua was physically separated from succoring Dinocrates in her vision, she could leap the chasm through prayer and the grace of God. It is also remarkable to have such an early account of a possibly unbaptized person achieving salvation (or a release from Purgatory—scholars argue this point) through the prayers of a believer, for it validates that this possibility was not condemned outright by the early Church, who protected, treasured, and widely distributed Perpetua's account.[12]

THE VISION OF COMBAT

Perpetua soon received another vision: Pomponius the deacon pounded on the gate of the prison, which Perpetua then unlatched for him. He was clothed in white, and led her through winding passages and rough terrain until she was standing, breathless, in the middle of an arena ringed with spectators. "Do not fear," Pomponius said, "I am here with you, and I am laboring with you!" She expected wild beasts to pour from the arena gates, but instead saw an Egyptian, frightful in

[11] One of Emperor Septimius Severus's sons. Upon his father's death in 211, he and his elder brother Caracalla shared power as co-emperors until Caracalla had him murdered later that year. His title of Caesar in the text denotes that the martyrs died before 209, when Geta became Augustus (Emperor). For more on Geta, see the images and text on the facing page.

[12] There was a belief at the time that imprisoned confessors of the Faith waiting to be martyred, such as Perpetua, could intercede and obtain salvation for the *lapsi* (those who had left the Faith) and pagans. For more, see *Heaven's Purge: Purgatory in Late Antiquity* by Isabel Moreira (Oxford University Press, 2010).

Coin of Septimius Severus, with Julia Domna, Caracalla, and Geta
Rome mint, struck in 202

Severan Tondo, 2nd century
Altes Museum, Berlin

These two objects are loaded with history and meaning. The coin and tondo both depict the emperor with his wife and two sons. The reverse of the coin shows his sons facing each other on either side of their mother, the words *Felicitas Saeculi* (The Age of Good Fortune) framing them. Caracalla would order his brother Geta's murder in the very arms of his mother, and then seek to efface his memory from history. This *damnatio memoriae* is seen on the tondo, where Geta's face has been scrubbed off and smeared with excrement.

appearance. Attendants came to strip and oil her for the upcoming wrestling match, and Perpetua was astonished to discover she had become a man. The Egyptian also stripped and rolled in the dust. An enormous man clothed in white and purple, towering higher than the walls of the arena, stepped into their midst. In one hand he held a rod carried by gladiator trainers; in the other, a green branch full of golden apples.

The towering giant called for silence, and his voice boomed across the land: "This Egyptian, if he should overcome this woman, shall kill her with the sword; and if she shall conquer him, she shall receive this branch." He departed, and they began the match. The two fought intensely, the Egyptian trying to trip her up and control her legs while Perpetua struck at his face. Finally, the Egyptian grabbed hold and lifted her into the air. Perpetua wrenched his head with her hands, causing the Egyptian to fall to the ground. She stomped upon his head as the spectators erupted in acclaim. The gigantic gladiator trainer handed her the branch with apples and, with a kiss, told her, "Daughter, peace be with you." As Perpetua triumphantly processed to the Sanavivarian Gate,[13] she woke up, now understanding that her fight would not be with the beasts, but with Satan himself.

The imagery of this vision, while fantastic, yields a rich theology of the actual combat that Perpetua and her companions would soon face. Their public struggle and martyrdom in the physical arena was but a shadow of the spiritual battle that would occur in the sight of saints, angels, demons, and God. Perpetua's transformation into a man is perhaps a reference to her having "put on Christ" [14] through her baptism, giving her the grace to resist the devil and his assaults. The oil she was anointed with, while a common part of wrestling matches in

[13] Literally, "gate of health" or "gate of salvation". This gate will play a part in their actual arena appearance.
[14] Galatians 3:27, Romans 13:14.

Greece and Rome, may also refer to the Oil of Catechumens that she and the others would have received at their baptism. They may have even heard a homily similar to the one that St. John Chrysostom (+A.D. 407) preached to his catechumens during their preparation:

> *So then, in your case these thirty days are like some wrestling school, both for exercise and practice: let us learn from thence already to get the better of that evil demon. For it is to contend with him that we have to strip ourselves, with him after baptism are we to box and fight. Let us learn from thence already his grip, on what side he is aggressive, on what side he can easily threaten us, in order that, when the contest comes on, we may not feel strange, nor become confused, as seeing new forms of wrestling; but having already practiced them among ourselves, and having learned all his methods, may engage in these forms of wrestling against him with courage.*[15]

The Egyptian, who signifies the devil who is forever outside the friendship of God, is not anointed with oil; rather, he rolled in the dust, an explicit reference to the curse God inflicted on Satan in Genesis 3:14: "Thou shalt crawl on thy belly and eat dust all thy life long." The dust is also a kind of curse in that it allowed Perpetua to get a better grip upon him. Wrestling under the watchful eye of the gigantic Christ, Perpetua crushed the head of the devil [16] and wins the branch of golden apples, which signifies the delights of the possession of God in Heaven.[17]

After recounting this vision, Perpetua wrote no more: "This, so far, I have completed several days before the exhibition; but what passed at

[15] Translated by T.P. Brandram. *Nicene and Post-Nicene Fathers, First Series*, Vol. 9. Edited by Philip Schaff. (Buffalo, NY: Christian Literature Publishing Co., 1889.) http://www.newadvent.org/fathers/1908.htm

[16] Genesis 3:15.

[17] Song of Songs 2:3, 5:1.

the exhibition itself let who will write." An unknown author took up the account at this point of the *Passio*.

FELICITY GIVES BIRTH

Saturus, the teacher of catechumens who had surrendered himself to the authorities so that he might remain with his students, also received a vision of Heaven. Soon after, Secundulus died in prison, thus "giving a respite to the beasts." The date of martyrdom was fast approaching, and the prisoners were tense with anticipation, especially the slave Felicity. She was now eight months pregnant, and unless she gave birth, she could not suffer with the others since the Romans would not execute a pregnant woman. She also feared that a delay would mean she would face death without the support of the other Christians and be executed among criminals and malefactors.

Three days before the games, sympathetic to Felicity's anxiety, the prisoners, "joining together their united cry, poured forth their prayer to the Lord." Immediately, Felicity went into labor. As she groaned in pain, a servant of one of the Roman soldiers taunted her: "You who are in such suffering now, what will you do when you are thrown to the beasts?" She replied, "Now it is I that suffer what I suffer; but then there will be another one in me, who will suffer for me, because I also am about to suffer for Him." She gave birth to a little girl, and gave her away for another to raise.

THE LAST SUPPER

The day before the arena shows, there was a tradition to hold a *cena libera*, or free meal, for the condemned and the gladiators. Similar to the modern practice of giving someone a final meal before their execution, the *cena libera* often degenerated into a riotous spectacle of drunkenness and gluttony, one last chance to indulge in pleasures of the flesh. St. Paul may have had these meals in mind when he wrote in 1 Corinthians 15:32, "When I fought against beasts at Ephesus with all my strength, of what use was it, if the dead do not rise again? Let us eat and drink, since we must die tomorrow." [18] Therefore, having hope that their impending struggle would result in eternal life, Perpetua, Felicity, and their companions chose instead to eat their *cena libera* in the manner of an *agape*—an evening liturgy that combined prayer and fraternal dining, normally separated from the celebration of the Eucharist.

As the onlookers jeered at and goaded the condemned, the Christians denounced the false beliefs of the crowd and exhorted them to convert before it was too late. Saturus raised his voice and said, "Tomorrow is not enough for you, that you might behold with pleasure the torment of that which you hate. Remember our faces, that you may recognize them on the day of judgment!" Astonished and chastened, the rabble departed, and "from these things many believed."

THE ARENA

The next day, the birthday of Emperor Severus's son Geta, the Christians proceeded from the prison to the amphitheater, "joyous and of brilliant countenances." The sight of the arena must have filled them with awe, for its only rival in size was the famous Flavian amphitheater in Rome. Built over a span of 200 years and intricately carved, the amphitheater in Carthage could seat some 30,000 spectators around its rectangular, racetrack design. Even its overgrown ruins could move

[18] Kyle, 108.

the hearts of sightseers, for 12th-century Arabs exclaimed that it had "no parallel in the entire world." [19]

The *Passio* describes Felicity as "rejoicing that she had safely brought forth [her child] so that she might fight with the wild beasts." As they neared the gate, servants handed them garments, for the men were to be clad as priests of Saturn and the women as those consecrated to Ceres. These garments were either a pagan mockery of Christianity or a way to offer sacrificial victims to Saturn and Ceres.

The Carthage Amphitheater, 1950

[19] Farina, 14.

The Carthage Amphitheater[20]

Regardless, the Christians refused to put them on. Perpetua declared that they have all freely consented to the judicial process, and it would be unjust to repay their respectfulness with this mockery. Surprisingly, the Tribune agreed, and the costumes were taken away. As William Farina of the excellent work *Perpetua of Carthage* noted, "Although the games were being held in honor of the birthday of the emperor's younger son, the sacrificial victims had thus far successfully co-opted the religious symbolism of the event in favor of the fledgling Christian community." [21] This theme of "co-opting" continued throughout the day; already, the crowds noticed that the prisoners were not behaving like the usual arena fodder. Instead of the typical displays of fear, begging, and piteous weeping, these condemned were joyous and confident.

[20] Photo by Neil Rickards, 2003 (CC Attribution 2.0, Generic).

[21] Farina, 15.

The martyrs continued their procession. Perpetua sang psalms, "already treading under foot the head of the Egyptian," while the men uttered threats to the gawking crowd. As they passed Hiliarianus the procurator, they said, "You judge us, but God will judge you!" The crowd became exasperated at this boldness and demanded that the prisoners be scourged as they processed past the *venatores*, the gladiators that hunted animals. Hiliarianus granted this request, and the Christians rejoiced that they got to share in the Lord's Passion as the *venatores* ruthlessly beat and whipped them.

Judicial executions were typically placed early in the schedule of festivities as a warm-up for the events to come. Revocatus, Saturninus, and Saturus entered the arena first. In the days before the games, they had all discussed how they would prefer to die. Saturninus, the one who had made such strong and incendiary comments to the crowds, said that he would like to face every beast at once so that his glory might be the greater. Saturus confided that he abhorred the thought of being mangled and methodically consumed by a bear; instead, he hoped he would gain death by the single bite of a leopard.

The animals began to enter the arena. A leopard and a bear attacked Revocatus and Saturninus, yet the text insinuates that they were only wounded by these animals and were dragged back to a gate for later execution.[22] Perhaps the beasts were not in the mood to kill, as some texts from the period describe martyrs having to goad the animals to attack. Indeed, when St. Ignatius of Antioch (+108) wrote to the Roman church on his way to martyrdom, he noted:

> *"I pray that they [the beasts] may be found eager to rush upon me, which also I will entice to devour me speedily, and not deal with me as*

[22] This may have been the Porta Libitinensis (Gate of Death), which is named after Libitina, the goddess of funerals.

with some, whom, out of fear, they have not touched. But if they be unwilling to assail me, I will compel them to do so." [23]

Saturus, in answer to his desire, did not have to face a bear; instead, the executioners tied him to a large boar. A huntsman then entered the arena to attack both boar and man, but the enraged boar turned on the hunter and gored him with its tusks; the huntsman died the next day from his wounds. The arena attendants next tried tying Saturus to the ground near a bear, but the bear refused to leave its cage. Unhurt, Saturus was recalled to the gate to join Revocatus and Saturninus.

The leaders of the games, possibly frustrated by their lack of success in killing the male criminals, decided to bring out Perpetua and Felicity. To match their feminine nature with a fitting animal, the attendants paired Perpetua and Felicity with a fierce cow. As the two women entered the arena, nude yet loosely clothed in nets, the crowd "[shuddered] as they [saw] one young woman of delicate frame, and another with breasts still dripping from her recent childbirth." Not wanting a lack of spectator enthusiasm at the games, the officials recalled Felicity and Perpetua, removed the nets, and clothed them more modestly before sending them out again.

The cow first charged Perpetua and hurled her into the air. She crashed into the arena floor and, in a daze, noticed that her tunic had been torn away from her legs, exposing her body to the crowd. Her trembling hand drew it back over her body, more "mindful of her modesty than her suffering." As she stood and bound up her disheveled hair out of dignity, she saw the rampaging cow crush and trample Felicity. Perpetua helped Felicity to her feet, and they were sent back

[23] Ignatius, *Letter to the Romans*, 5, in Maxwell Staniforth, ed. and tr., *Early Christian Writings: The Apostolic Fathers*, rev. Andrew Louth (Harmondsworth: Penguin Books, 1987).

to the Sanavivarian Gate[24] to be executed later, as the thirst of the crowd was slaked for the time being. As the women waited for their next combat, Perpetua appeared to come out of an ecstasy, saying, "I cannot tell when we are to be led out to that cow." It was only when she saw her wounds that she understood what had occurred. Her brother and another catechumen named Rusticus tended to the two injured women, and Perpetua said, "Stand fast in the faith, and love one another, all of you, and be not offended at my sufferings."

THE EXECUTION

At the other gate, the unwounded Saturus spoke with Pudens, the warden of the prison: "Up to this moment, I have felt no beast. And now believe with your whole heart…I shall be destroyed with one bite of the leopard." As the conclusion of the exhibition arrived, Saturus entered the arena and was set upon by that same leopard. He may have been affixed to a wheeled cart, as depicted in the mosaic on page 48. The cat sank its teeth into his neck and a torrent of blood flooded over his body. In an unknowing profession of this "second baptism" of blood,[25] the crowd crowed, "Well washed! Well washed, indeed!" As Saturus lay dying, he spoke again to the warden Pudens, who was in awe of his prisoners' behavior and had treated them as kindly as possible. "Farewell," Saturus told him, "and be mindful of my faith; let not these things disturb, but confirm you." He took a little ring from the finger of Pudens, dipped it in his blood, and handed it back as a memory and relic of his sufferings. The words and action of Saturus are

[24] This same gate was the one seen by Perpetua in her vision of combat with the Egyptian, where she walked out of the gate in victory. Now, she will go forth one more time from this "Gate of Salvation" to eternal life.
[25] It is an ancient belief of the Church that unbaptized persons who died as martyrs for the Faith could still find salvation by this baptism of blood. Saturus was already baptised by water, so this was a kind of symbolic second baptism.

a strong indication that Pudens converted to Christianity. Regardless, executioners dragged Saturus onto the pile of injured victims who were waiting for their coup de grâce.

The crowd was now eager to watch each criminal's execution so that "they might make their eyes partners in the murder." Those of the condemned who could still walk moved to the place of execution, exchanging with one another a final kiss of peace. Those in the pile of the grievously injured, including Saturus, had already been run through with a sword. Just as in Perpetua's vision of the ladder, Saturus had made the climb first.

The killing proceeded normally as each received the sword thrust "immovable and in silence." The gladiator who approached Perpetua was young, inexperienced, and nervous. His blow missed the mark and hit bone, and Perpetua cried out in pain. She took his shaking hand in her own, helped align his sword to her throat, and he killed her cleanly. Thus ends the *Passio*.

After their deaths, the story of what happened in Carthage quickly spread among the Christians of North Africa, and the *Passio* became incredibly popular, even to the point where some communities professed that it was inspired scripture of the same importance as the letters of St. Paul. There was no official New Testament canon of scripture for the universal Church until the late 4th century, so the *Passio* joined various other apocalypses, gospels, and epistles as churches distributed these writings throughout the empire.

The cult of the six martyrs also expanded with great rapidity. By 354, the Roman Philocalian Calendar included their names, and the

Mosaic from Dar Buc Ammera villa depicting the condemned in a wheeled cart, dated to before 80 A.D.

Jamahiriya Museum, Tripoli, Libya

A leopard attacks in this mosaic from the 3rd century A.D.

Museum of El Djem, Tunisia

Copyright Rached Msadek

The martyrdom of Perpetua (lower right), Felicity (upper right), and their companions, c. 1000

From the *Menalogion of Basil II*, Vatican Library

Eastern Syriac Calendar soon followed.[26] Interestingly, the names of Perpetua and Felicity came to identify the group as a whole, and the Roman Canon of the Mass only mentions the two women.

A splendid church, the Basilica Maiorum, was built over the martyrs' tombs and may have been the most famous church in North Africa. Archaeological digs in the ruins of the basilica have yielded fragments bearing Perpetua's family name of Vibii, which indicates that it may have been her family's burial plot. One fragment reads *Perpetue Filie Dulcissimae* (Ever sweet daughter) and dates from the third century. As Farina touchingly notes, "While any identification is speculation, one is tempted to think of the last affectionate memory

[26] Farina, 58.

of Perpetua from her parents from whom she had so violently estranged herself." [27]

St. Augustine of Hippo mentioned this basilica in his sermons on the feast day of Perpetua and Felicity, and he related with some distress the carnival atmosphere that had taken hold of the feast day. By this time (the late 4th century) schism had fractured the North African churches into fiercely opposed factions, and the coming fall of the Roman Empire would drop like a hammer blow. While the Eastern Roman (Byzantine) Empire was able to gain control of North Africa and bring some stability, it collapsed under a tidal wave of Islamic conquest that crested in France and was bloodily rolled back to Spain.

Crusaders attempted to take back the region but could not maintain a foothold. St. Louis IX of France, leading one of the last crusades, died in Carthage. Seemingly, Christianity in North Africa had finally perished in the place where the martyrs had so nobly professed it. Carthage remained in Muslim hands, and earned the following ignoble distinction from Edward Gibbon: "The northern coast of Africa is the only land in which the light of the Gospel, after a long and perfect establishment, has been totally extinguished."

While their bodies slept in the tombs long neglected, the martyrs' names and deeds were kept alive wherever the Church spread. Yet, like her tomb, Perpetua's first-hand account in the *Passio* lay hidden for centuries. Until the *Passio*'s rediscovery at the Abbey of Monte Cassino in 1661, the primary sources of information on the martyrs were the rather unimaginative and short tales found in devotional materials such as Jacobus de Voragine's *Golden Legend.* When it finally came to light,

[27] Farina, 228-229.

Mary and Child with Saints Felicity and Perpetua

c. 1520

National Museum, Warsaw

the raw and personal *Passio* was a sensation and ignited the imagination of authors and artists.

The 19th century brought another attempt to convert North Africa, this time by a French community known as the White Fathers. Their work may not have resulted in a blossoming of Christianity in Carthage, but they did bring forth archaeological wonders. In 1907, Fr. DeLattre of the White Fathers, an expert in early Roman archaeology, was digging in the ruins of the Basilica Maiorum. Picking through the rubble, he noticed what appeared to be fragments from a shattered inscription. He sorted and arranged the pieces until, incredibly, the names of Perpetua, Felicity, and their companions appeared. Pieces of bone and religious items brought further testimony that this was the final resting place of the martyrs. The written *Passio* joined archaeological evidence to produce what is arguably the most vivid account of martyrdom from the ancient world.

Saints Felicity and Perpetua, *pray for us*.

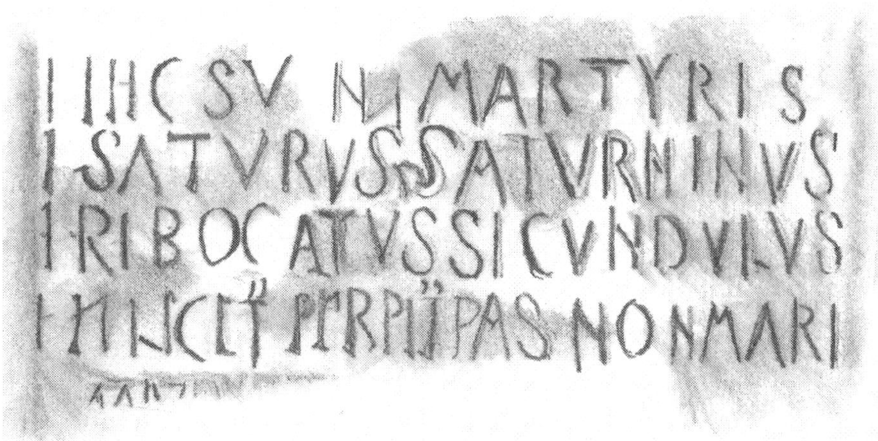

The inscription discovered by Fr. DeLattre in Carthage's Basilica Maiorum. Drawing by author.

"Here are the martyrs Saturus, Saturninus, Revocatus, Secundulus, Felicitas, Perpetua, who suffered on the Nones (7th) of March" [28]

[28] Susan Raven, *Rome in Africa* (London: Evans Brothers Limited, 1969), 120.

AGATHA

Martyred *in approximately 251 A.D. in Catania, Sicily*

Feast Day*—February 5th*

How lovely are thy palms, Agatha! But how long and cruel was thy combat for them! The day was thine; thy faith and thy virginity triumphed, but the battlefield streamed with thy blood, and thy glorious wounds bear testimony to the angels how stern was the courage of thy fidelity to Jesus thy Spouse.

Dom Prosper Gueranger[1]

On the middle of the eastern coast of Sicily, where the land tucks gently inwards, is the city of Catania. It is an ancient habitation, though it lies beneath the ever-threatening Mount Etna, a volcano that has devastated the area at least 17 times throughout the centuries. During one particularly destructive eruption in 1669 A.D., Catania's walls saved its citizens by diverting the lava; 24 years later, an earthquake flattened the city. Greeks, Romans, and Arabs conquered and settled it; Vandals sacked it; and Allied bombers devastated it during World War II. Throughout much of this glorious, violent history, Catania's patron saint rested within its walls, keeping vigil over the land where she met her violent end.

[1] Abbot Gueranger, *The Liturgical Year - Septuagesima*, tr. by Dom Laurence Shepherd (London: Burns and Oates, Ltd., 1909), 244.

Saint Agatha

After Massimo Stanzione, 1585-1656

Image courtesy of Skinner, Inc. (www.skinnerinc.com)

Though St. Agatha is one of the most important and celebrated saints of the early Church, there is little historical certainty about her life and death. Much of what is known about her stems from the *Acta* written no earlier than the 6th century, and it is difficult to discern legend from fact. Such is the case for many of the early saints, as centuries of veneration and imagination have accreted into rich, sometimes maddeningly contradictory, portraits of their lives. And yet, this book is not an exercise in historical criticism, but a work of devotion and gratitude. Therefore, I will follow the same method as in my earlier work on St. Mary Magdalene, *Like a Dove in the Cleft of the Rock*: "I believe that it is possible to draw upon all of these stories and legends about her in order to look at the spiritual lessons that they teach. The strictness of the scholar is not necessary here, as we wish to call upon the whole panoply of art, literature, and piety." [1]

From the very beginning, St. Agatha's story is controversial: both Palermo and Catania claim that she was born in their city, and declare her as their patron (though Catania holds the most substantial portion of her relics in its cathedral). Yet, both cities agree that she died in Catania. In this matter, it is best to take the advice of famed 18th-century hagiographer Alban Butler: "The cities of Palermo and Catania, in Sicily, dispute the honour of her birth; but they do much better who, by copying her virtues, and claiming her patronage, strive to become her fellow-citizens in heaven." [2]

According to the 13th-century *Golden Legend,*[3] a famous volume of lives of the saints, Agatha was 15 years old, "right fair, noble of body and of heart, and was rich of goods. This glorious virgin served God in the city of Catania, leading a pure and holy life." In the early days of the

[1] Page 30.
[2] https://www.ewtn.com/library/MARY/AGATHA.HTM
[3] De Voragine, Jacobus, *The Golden Legend (as Englished by William Caxton, Volume III)*, edited by F.S. Ellis (London: J.M. Dent and Co., 1900), 33.

Church, it was common for devout young women to vow themselves as virgins to a life of prayer and singular devotion to God, a practice stemming from St. Paul's exhortations in 1 Corinthians 7. Her life might have been lived out in peace and obscurity were it not for the Prefect Quintianus. He was a local administrator whom the *Golden Legend* describes as "being of a low lineage…lecherous, avaricious, and a miscreant." [4]

Quintianus relentlessly pursued Agatha, but she refused to be swayed from her vow of virginity. Exasperated, he called her to stand before him and offer sacrifice to idols of the pagan gods. Perhaps he reasoned that faced with the choice to offer sacrifice or die, Agatha would save her life by turning her back on her belief in Christ's love which undergirded her chastity. Once that bulwark was thrown down, it would be a simple matter to pressure her into giving up all. However, she stood firm and refused to offer any sacrifices to the pagan idols. Quintianus ordered that Agatha should be forced to live for 30 days with a notorious brothel keeper named Aphrodesia, whose nine daughters were "over foul, like unto the mother." [5] If Agatha's steadfastness could not be broken through threats, perhaps she would be pulled down through an unremitting exposure to vice and temptation.

Each day, Aphrodesia and her daughters would entice Agatha with descriptions of all that she would gain if only she would give in to Quintianus's demands. Then, seeing that she was still set in her resolve, they would change tactics and berate and torment her by describing the terrible punishments and sufferings she would soon experience if she remained obstinate. At this point, the *Golden Legend* begins to use

[4] Ibid.

[5] Ibid.

Saint Agatha
Bergognone, 1510
Accadémie de Carare, Bergame, Italy

dialogue as Agatha replies to her female tormenters, and all further dialogue will come from that ancient source:[6]

> *"My courage and my thoughts are so firmly founded upon the solid stone of Jesus Christ, that no pain will alter my resolve; your words are wind, your promises like the rain that drains away, and your menaces like rivers that quickly pass along. No matter how violently all these things tear at the foundation of my courage, it shall not be moved."*[7]

Agatha refused to capitulate, but spent her time in prayer and tears, begging God for the grace to be a faithful martyr if that was His will. At the end of 30 days, Aphrodesia went to Quintianus in frustration, and reported:

> *"Sooner should the stones wax soft, and iron turn to soft lead, than we might turn the courage of this maid, or take from her the Christian faith. My daughters and I have done no other thing night and day, one day after another, but work at how we might turn her heart to your desires."*

At this, Quintianus called Agatha to stand before him in judgment. He ordered her to sacrifice to idols and cast aside the faith that gave her such determination. She answered that she would never bow to these so-called gods that, in truth, are demons. Driven to force his hand, Quintianus put forth his final challenge: "Sacrifice to the gods or die in torment." In a marvelous exchange, Agatha taunted him:

> *"Hah! You say these are gods; therefore, your wife must long to conduct her life after the impure and adulterous Venus, and you must take after that murderer Jupiter!"*

[6] The archaic English of the edited 15th-century version used below has been modernized and adapted for clarity.
[7] De Voragine, 33.

"Oh," Quintianus replied, "you'd better believe that you will suffer torments now since you dare to throw such insults at me!"

"Well, how can I not be amazed that such a wise man as yourself has become a fool! For you worship such despicable gods, yet neither you nor your wife will follow their example! If your gods are good, then I would hope you would conform your lives to theirs; if evil, then you and I agree that they deserve no worship."[8]

At this, the frustrated Quintianus made one last appeal, but Agatha refused to sacrifice. He sent her to "a dark prison, and she went as gladly as she would have gone to her wedding."

The next morning, Quintianus had Agatha brought before him. He asked:

"Agatha, how are you feeling? How is your health?"

"Christ is my health."

"Deny Christ your God, and you'll escape your torments."

"No, you deny your filthy idols of stone and wood and adore your true Maker who created the heavens and the earth. If not, you will burn in the eternal fires of Hell."[9]

Quinaianus ordered that Agatha be stretched on a rack. This torture was often accompanied by whipping, raking the body with iron hooks, and burning the wounds. As she suffered, he again offered to stop the torture if she would recant. She said,

"I have welcomed this pain with the joy of him who covets something and finally sees it, or he who has discovered a great treasure and finally claims it. And like the wheat that may not rest in the granary until the chaff has been beaten off, in the same way, my soul may not

[8] Ibid., 34.
[9] Ibid., 35.

> *enter the realm of heaven until it has suffered at the hands of your torturers."* [10]

Quintianus then directed the torturers to tear and cut off Agatha's breasts. This is one of the most shocking and incomprehensible violations in all the accounts of martyrdom. Throughout the centuries, artists have carefully depicted this particular torture in devotional artwork of St. Agatha, and it strikes the modern observer as unsettling and strange. Is the focus on her breasts due to an underlying sexual/sadistic fascination? Are they showing her abuse as an example of male dominance over women? Such questions are indeed valid, and it is worth taking the time to understand the historical background of this theme.

Anne Ashton's doctoral thesis for the University of St. Andrews, *Interpreting Breast Iconography in Italian Art 1250-1600*, exhaustively investigates the reasons for the often-shocking portrayals of the nude breast in devotional and profane artwork of times past. Ashton begins her assessment by reminding the modern reader that he is viewing a work that is hundreds of years removed from its intended audience; hence, his judgments and reactions to its contents may not be the same as those of its original audience.[11] Whereas a modern viewer may initially notice the nudity of St. Agatha in, say, an illuminated manuscript's depiction of her torture, the medieval audience would be drawn to her sacrifice not only of her life, but of her motherhood, youth, and beauty.[12] As Ashton explains:

[10] Ibid., 35.
[11] Ashton, 17.
[12] Ibid., 32.

St. Agatha's mutilation and imprisonment, c. 1000
From the *Menalogion of Basil II*, Vatican Library

The torture of St. Agatha, before 1256
Stained glass Bay 109, panel C2 in the cathedral of St. Julian, Le Mans

> *Agatha was reduced to the lowest physical state, but like Mary and Christ on the cross, this state is an expression of her power. Stripped and battered she constituted a symbol of hope which was enhanced by the fact that it was her breasts which had been attacked; in themselves symbols not only of her chastity but also her womanhood and possible motherhood and a link to the Virgin Mary. Cult images of Agatha and passion plays narrating her story gave crowds a visual experience which was designed to increase their horror and therefore their wonder and enhance their religious devotion. To reduce these images to mere sado-pornography is a mistake.*[13]

However, the early Renaissance and changing cultural mores brought about nudity in art that was more open to erotic interpretation, especially since many patrons were commissioning works for their private collections. A comparison of a medieval illumination of St. Agatha's breast torture against Sebastiano del Piombo's *Martyrdom of Saint Agatha* makes the point quite clearly. Del Piombo's Agatha is a model of polished renaissance beauty, nude to the waist, and her torturers appear almost gentle with their tongs. This type of ambivalently erotic artwork, especially when it was depicting a holy person and intended for public viewing, was soon restricted by ecclesiastical authorities, and subsequent works usually portrayed Agatha fully clothed, sometimes with her severed breasts resting on a nearby platter.[14]

Still, the question remains: Why were devotional images of Agatha undergoing the torture of her breasts so popular, such that this particular suffering became a symbol of the saint, rather than the other agonies and events of her martyrdom? For many of the early female martyrs, the exposure and/or torture of their breasts was a common occurrence. Part of the cruel designs of the authorities was the

[13] Ibid., 33.
[14] Ibid., 33-34.

humiliation of the martyrs' beliefs, especially when their victim was a young virgin who had chosen a life of celibacy. Because breasts are a symbol of maternity and a sex identifier, they were a focus for humiliation and torture, along with the overall violation of the virgin's desire for modesty.[15] This degradation of their sex and convictions became symbolic of the outrages committed against Christ, in imitation of whom they were willing to suffer. As the centuries passed and devotional artwork focused more on the sufferings and torture of Christ, it was only natural that artists would show these saints in the throes of their most memorable tortures, united with their Model and Head. Hence, St. Agatha's forced mastectomy became the touchstone symbol of her martyrdom.[16]

Returning to the *Golden Legend*'s account of St. Agatha's passion, her torturers having finished cutting off her breasts, she said to Quintianus,

> *"Cruel tyrant, do you have no shame? You cut off from a woman that with which your mother gave you suck and nourishment. Regardless, my breasts are whole within my soul, and they nourish the life I have given to Jesus Christ."*[17]

The guards dragged her back into her cell, and none could enter to treat her horrible wounds, let alone give her food and water.

That night, an elderly, distinguished man carrying jars of ointments and salves entered her cell. A young child walked before him, lighting their way. The man said,

> *"Agatha, I am a surgeon. That foul man has terribly wounded your body, but your courage and answers have more grievously torn his*

[15] Ibid., 165.
[16] Ibid., 188-189.
[17] De Voragine, 35-36.

heart. I was there when your breasts were torn off, and I know how to heal them."

"Sir, I have never had recourse to physicians, and I do not wish to begin now. I have offered Christ everything, and I don't wish to take anything back that has been given in these torments."

"Dearest Agatha," the old man replied, "I too am a Christian and a wise physician, so have no shame in allowing me to heal your breasts."

"Why should I be ashamed? You are very old, and even though I am young, my beauty has been wrecked by those men. Nevertheless, God has allowed this, so there is no need for you to ease my pain. I have Jesus Christ, Who with a word can heal any man's wounds. If He desires it, He will heal mine."

Saint Agatha visited in prison by Saint Peter and the angel
Giovanni Lanfranco, c. 1614
National Gallery of Parma

> *With a smile, the old man said, "He does desire it. For He has sent me, his Apostle, to you. In His name, you are whole."*
>
> *At this, Agatha fell to the floor in prayer, crying, "Oh, Lord Jesus Christ, I thank you that you have remembered me, sending your Apostle St. Peter to visit me and heal my wounds." Rising, she saw that her breasts were healed and whole and the entire prison was filled with radiant, pure light. All the jailers fled in confusion and dread, and the cell doors stood open. The other prisoners exhorted her to escape into hiding, but she refused to condemn her guards to punishment if she left. She remained in her cell to finish earning her crown.*[18]

Four days later, Quintianus yet again brought Agatha before him, exhorting her to sacrifice.

> *"Your words," she replied, "are vain and evil, and they foul the very air you use to utter them. How can you be so wicked as to persist in calling upon a dumb stone to save you, and resist the Lord that has healed me and restored my breasts?"*
>
> *"Tell me truthfully who has healed you, Agatha."*
>
> *"Jesus Christ."*
>
> *"You still call upon that name?"*
>
> *"I call upon him in my heart as long as I live."*
>
> *"Well, let's observe for ourselves if he can help and heal you."*[19]

He ordered her torturers to remove her clothes and force her to roll upon burning coals. At this, the ground quaked and trembled, and a deep groaning came from the earth. A section of wall collapsed upon Silvian, Quintianus's counselor; another smashed Fastian, the man who was responsible for suggesting her tortures. The earthquake shook the entire city of Catania, and the people fled their homes, begging

[18] Ibid., 36-37.
[19] Ibid., 37.

Saint Agatha
Lorenzo Lippi, 1638/1644
Blanton Museum of Art, Austin

Quintianus to stop tormenting the saint. Fearing the mob and surrounded by the corpses of his friends, he ordered that Agatha, now near death, be once again taken to her cell. In her prison, before the eyes of many onlookers outside, Agatha summoned the last reserves of her strength. She fell to her knees, joined and raised her hands to Heaven, and prayed:

> *"Lord God Jesus Christ, who created me from nothing, and since my youth have protected me and allowed me to live well, you took from my heart the love of the world and gave me the strength to endure my torments. You gave me patience in my pain, and I now pray that you take my spirit, for it is time for me to leave this world and come to your mercy."* [20]

Her prayer finished, she gave up her soul on February 5th, "in the year of our Lord two hundred and fifty-three in the time of Decius, the emperor of Rome." [21] Her grieving friends took up her body, anointed it, and prepared it for burial. As they were working, a young man clothed in silk, followed by a hundred others wearing rich garments, stationed themselves by the tomb. The townspeople had never seen these men before, but they continued with the funeral and laid her body in the tomb. The mysterious young man placed a marble tablet at her head:

MENTEM SANCTAM, SPONTANEAM, HONOREM DEO DEDIT ET PATRIAE LIBERATIONEM FECIT [22]

[20] Ibid., 38.

[21] Ibid.

[22] "Holy in thought, freely giving honor to God in all she did, liberating her nation."

The group of men never returned, leading many to believe that the young man who led them was her guardian angel who brought a cohort to give her honor.

As news of these marvelous things spread throughout the countryside, even Jews and pagan Saracens came to St. Agatha's tomb to praise her with song and beseech her help. Quintianus reportedly never gave up attempting to ruin Agatha's family and defile her name, and soon after died a horrible death.

A year after Agatha's passion, a terrible fire, perhaps a lava flow from Mount Etna, broke out in the mountains surrounding Catania and consumed even the earth and stones. As the inferno drew near the city, some pagans ran to her tomb and grabbed her burial cloth. They held it up in the direction of the oncoming flames, and the fire subsided. It was February 5th, St. Agatha's feast day, and all rejoiced that the young man's tablet spoke the truth—she is indeed the protectress and liberator of her nation.

Its story told, the *Golden Legend* ends with a prayer:

> *To glorious St. Agatha, we pray that she may beseech and obtain the grace to be kept from all perils of fire in this world, and from the perpetual fire of the world to come, that we might come to the glory and joy of Heaven. Amen.*

St. Agatha's renown quickly spread throughout the empire. The ancient martyrologies of the Latin and Greek churches speak of her, and Carthage added her name to the Canon of the Mass as early as 530. Numerous churches were built in her honor. Even after her death, St. Agatha continues to be a protectress of her nation. The eruptions and lava flows of Mount Etna are always a lingering threat, and several times the inhabitants took the veil of St. Agatha from her tomb and processed it around Catania to save the people from destruction.

St. Agatha's Silver Reliquary [23]
Giovanni di Bartolo, 1376
Catania Cathedral

Sicilians credit her with twice driving out Muslim invaders, and her body temporarily rested in Constantinople in the 11th century so that she might bless and protect that city from harm. In 1127, the Byzantines brought her remains back to Catania and interred her in the cathedral that bears her name. There, she rests to this day.[24]

Saint Agatha, *pray for us.*

[23] Photo by 199341G (CC 4.0).
[24] Butler, Alban, "St. Agatha", *The Lives of the Saints*, https://www.bartleby.com/210/2/051.html

LUCY

Martyred *in 304 A.D. in Syracuse, Sicily*

Feast Day*—December 13th*

Now, blessed Lucy, called light *or* light's way, *to whom the Holy Ghost gave such great strength by a unique property of special grace that a thousand men could not drag you to the brothel, even with many a pair of oxen: grant us to be so strong in virtue that no vice can damage us.*

Osbern Bokenkam, *A Legend of Holy Women*[1]

Even though St. Agatha had been resting in her tomb at Catania for over 50 years, her name and story continued their travels throughout the Empire. Her courage and fidelity to the Lord made her a heroic example, especially to the women of Sicily, and miraculous stories of her intercession abounded.

One warm, peerless day in the year 303 A.D., a small cluster of pilgrims processed through the streets of Catania. They kept a low profile, for the Emperor Diocletian was seeking the destruction of the Church in a focused, all-encompassing manner that had not been seen in the persecutions of his predecessors. The little group was from Syracuse and had traveled 50 miles along the eastern coast to pay St.

[1] Bokenham, Osbern, *A Legend of Holy Women*, tr. by Sheila Delany (Notre Dame, IN: University of Notre Dame Press, 1992), 167.

Saint Lucy
Domenico di Pace Beccafumi, 1521
Pinacoteca Nazionale, Bologna

Agatha a visit. Among them was a wealthy Greek woman named Eutychia. Beside her walked her daughter, Lucy.[2]

Eutychia had been suffering from a severe hemorrhage for four years, and this caused her great anxiety. For not only was she concerned about her own health, but her husband had died when Lucy was quite young, and while she had finally found Lucy a match (and forced a betrothal), her daughter seemed to be disinterested in the upcoming marriage. At times, Eutychia even suspected that Lucy was trying to intentionally delay her wedding. With her money draining away to doctors and Lucy now twenty years old, something had to be done. At the prompting of her daughter, Eutychia decided to make a pilgrimage to the relics of St. Agatha and ask for healing.

They soon arrived at St. Agatha's tomb. As they knelt in prayer, Lucy's heart was in turmoil. When she was very young, she had made a secret vow to give her heart completely to God as a virgin. When her mother pressed the match to a young pagan man, she could see that marriage would help relieve her widowed mother of her money concerns, but how could she break her promise to God? Time was running out—one way or another, the truth would have to burst forth, but what wreckage would result? What would become of her? Lucy's heart poured out her longings to St. Agatha, begging her to pray that the Lord would keep her faithful no matter what the future held.

Kneeling next to her daughter, Eutychia grimaced in agony as another spasm began to course its way throughout her damaged tissues. The long journey had not been kind to her body, and she felt faint from

[2] Unless otherwise cited, the following dramatized account is derived from Bokenham's *Legend of Holy Women* and the Catholic Encyclopedia article on St. Lucy: Bridge, James. "St. Lucy", *The Catholic Encyclopedia. Vol. 9.* (New York: Robert Appleton Company, 1910). http://www.newadvent.org/cathen/09414a.htm

Two depictions of Lucy and Eutychia's visit to St. Agatha's tomb. The upper, part of an altarpiece by Giovanni di Bartolommeo Cristiani in the Metropolitan Museum of Art (late 14th century), depicts an angelic host; the lower, part of the *Speculum historiale* by Jean de Vignay (late 15th century, Bibliothèque Nationale de France), shows St. Agatha in the midst of the angels.

her loss of blood over the past few days. "Oh St. Agatha, help me!" she groaned. As the pain intensified, it transformed into an odd sensation of warmth and deep relief. Her nausea and lightheadedness melted away, and she knew that something had changed. As they both rose to leave, Lucy noticed that her mother did not grasp her arm for support.

"Lucy," Eutychia said, "let's take a walk."

"Mother, is everything all right? Are you sure you don't need to go back and rest?"

"No need, I feel very well right now. As I was praying, I was in horrible pain, but it went away, and I feel so much better. I don't want to presume anything, but is it possible I may have been healed?"

Before she knew what she was saying, Lucy told her mother about her vow and her desire to give her dowry to the poor. They stood in silence, gazing at a new group of pilgrims walking to the young virgin's tomb. Eutychia reached over, took Lucy's hand, and said, "Let's go pay Agatha another visit." That night, Lucy dreamt that St. Agatha took her hands and said, "Soon you shall be the glory of Syracuse, as I am of Catania."

During the rest of their stay in Catania and on the journey home, Eutychia did not bleed. She was convinced that she had been healed through the intercession of St. Agatha, but doubt would sometimes crowd out her peace and disturb her sleep. Each morning she would nervously check for spots of blood, but everything would be clean.

One morning, they were sitting in the shade, watching as a flock of gulls caught the breeze out to sea. "Lucy, I think it's time that I make a decision about your wedding. We can't stall any longer." Lucy's stomach churned with sudden anxiety. Eutychia continued, "Seeing that you're promised to Another of great wealth and influence, how can I stand in the way of that union? You have my blessing. Do what you will with the dowry."

Saint Lucy with Jesus and Mary
c. 1290
Santa Lucia dei Giaconelli, Melfi, Italy

Stunned, Lucy could only whisper, “Oh Mother, thank you.”

The rest of the week brought great excitement and activity not only to Lucy and Eutychia’s household but throughout their neighborhood. Word quickly spread that Lucy was selling her jewels and elegant clothing, and had already given her vast dowry to the poor. When her fiancé heard that she was breaking her engagement and had cast away her fortune, he was consumed with rage. It was one thing for him to allow Lucy to indulge her weak, womanly religion by taking a trip to visit a grave. It was another thing entirely when it put poisonous ideas in her head and drove her to fanaticism.

The young man's father arranged a meeting with the local governor, Paschasius. Lucy was formally denounced as a Christian, which required the governor to act in accord with Diocletian's decrees. Soldiers apprehended her and brought her before the governor. Paschasius peered down at this beautiful young woman and said, "Lucy, you are accused of being a Christian and of living contrary to the laws of our emperors, bringing shame to your ancestry. If it is true, you are to blame, so if you will avoid humiliation and injury, be a wise woman and sacrifice to our gods, meekly offering them frankincense."

Raising her head, Lucy retorted, "A true and immaculate sacrifice is made this way to God, the Father of Heaven: when a person takes pleasure in visiting fatherless children and comforting the troubled. Since I now have nothing else but myself to bring as a humble sacrifice to the Father of Heaven, I offer myself as His sacrifice, ready to die for His sake."

Paschasius rolled his eyes, absently tapped his finger on the table, and said, "Perhaps this little virgin would find a brothel a more suitable place to live out her faith. She can remain there until she's dead from fatigue." [3]

The soldiers attempted to march her to a nearby house of prostitution, but she was rooted in place by the Holy Spirit, impossible to move. Some artistic depictions of this scene show her roped to a team of straining oxen, stressing either a bizarre attempt by the men to overcome her or to symbolically depict the power of the divine intervention that kept a slight young woman unharmed and unmoved.

Whether the attempt involved men, oxen, horses, or anything else, Lucy was not going anywhere. Exasperated, Paschasius sputtered, "Very well, you'll die where you stand. Burn her!" The soldiers heaped

[3] Bokenham, 170,172.

great piles of wood and pitch around Lucy as the growing crowd of onlookers jeered or pleaded for mercy. Her mother openly wept, but she caught her breath as Lucy's countenance transformed. She was still a young woman, but her face took on an otherworldly nobility as if she had come from a place of transcendent wisdom and tranquility. As the flame was set to the wood, Lucy turned her eyes, which now appeared both ancient and newborn, to her mother.

With a tremendous roar, the fire consumed the pitch and turpentine-soaked wood, driving the crowd back with its incredible heat. As the flames died down, they were astonished to see Lucy standing in the middle of the charred, smoking wood, her clothing unsinged. Trembling with fear and rage, Paschasius could not tear his gaze away from Lucy's eyes, which seemed to peer deep within his heart and find him wanting. He blindly grabbed at the shoulder of the guard next to him and screamed, "Cut out her eyes! Blind her and put an end to this torment!" The soldier, to the gasps and cries of the crowd, blinded Lucy and then plunged his dagger into her throat.

As the blood poured from her ruined face and neck, she cried out, "I have a word from God! This persecution will soon end, and peace will come for the Church. Emperor Diocletian will die in his sin, but not before you, Paschasius, are found out by Rome for all your treason, theft, and falsity. Then, the axe will come and hasten you home to Hell." [4] At this, she commended her soul to God and died. It was December 13, 304. As her body was being prepared for burial, her family was astonished to see that her eyes had been restored.

[4] "Hasten you home…" – a wonderful turn of phrase by the translator of Bokenham, page 174. Bokenham reported that Paschasius was executed for theft of funds.

Saint Lucy before the Judge (detail)
Lorenzo Lotto, 1532
Pinacoteca Civica "Francesco Podesti", Ancona, Italy

Emperor Diocletian abdicated his throne in 305 A.D., and persecutions trickled to a halt in the western Empire, finally ceasing when Constantine rose to power. With peace having come to the Church at last, Syracuse built a fitting basilica for St. Lucy over the place of her martyrdom. As St. Agatha had promised, the people of

Syracuse had taken Lucy to their heart as their own patron saint, just as Agatha represented nearby Catania.

It is fitting to end this chapter with the same words that the medieval author Bokenham used to conclude his account of Lucy's martyrdom:

> *[She is now] awaiting the great judgment day. On that day, O Lucy, I humbly beg that the translator of your legend may for his labors (by mediation of you who are called 'light' according to your name) have a glimpse of him who is the sun of righteousness and who illumines everyone with his grace. To see him once is joy. Amen and thank you Jesus.*[5]

Saint Lucy, *pray for us.*

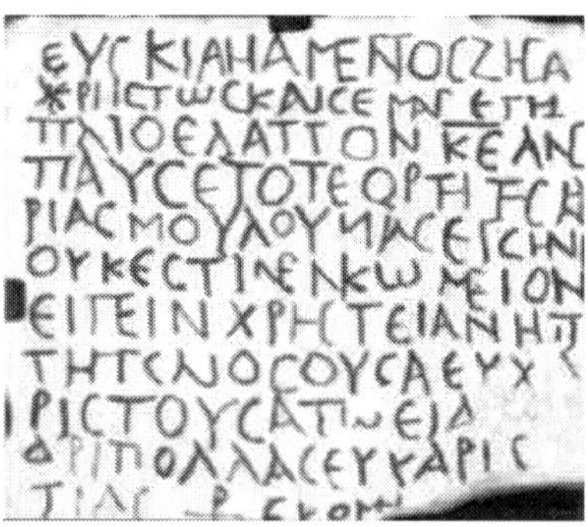

This Greek inscription was discovered in 1894 in the Catacomb of St. John in Syracuse. Dating from the late 4th century, it is the burial dedication of a husband to his deceased wife, Euschia. It is the earliest known evidence of devotion to St. Lucy.

Translation:

Euschia the virtuous, who lived honestly and nobly for about 25 years, died on the feast day of my Lady Lucia, whom it is unnecessary to praise. Perfect, devout Christian, pleased her husband by her many graces, courteous.[6]

[5] Ibid.

[6] Jeremy Dummett, *Syracuse, City of Legends: A Glory of Sicily* (eBook) (London: 2010).

Saint Lucy
with the kind permission of
Neilson Carlin, ©2018
www.neilsoncarlin.com

AGNES

Martyred *in 304* A.D. *in Rome*

Feast Day*—January 21st*

With her relics gathered here,
The altar o'er them placed revere,
She beneath God's feet reposes,
Nor to us her soft eye closes,
Nor her gracious ear

Prudentius, *Peristephanon*[1]

"When the Diocletian persecution was at its height, and when priests as well as laymen were apostatizing from the faith, Agnes, a girl of twelve, freely chose to die for Christ." [2] So the Passionist nuns described the courage and fidelity of the next martyr named in the Canon, St. Agnes. She was a Roman girl who came from a wealthy and influential family, and the fullest blessings and promises of worldly life lay before her when she chose to sacrifice them for the sake of Jesus Christ.

[1] Wiseman, Cardinal Nicholas Patrick, *Fabiola; Or, The Church of the Catacombs* (New York: Benziger Brothers, 1886), 251.
[2] https://www.passionistnuns.org/Saints/StAgnes/index.htm, accessed 3/13/2018.

Saint Agnes

Master of the Dutuit Mount of Olives, late 15th century

Rijksmuseum, Amsterdam

In 291 A.D., a noble Christian family of Rome welcomed a baby girl into the world. They gave her the name Agnes, which in its Greek form calls forth images of purity, reverence, and piety. As the years passed, a beauty both physical and interior radiated forth from this young woman, causing numerous influential young men to express an interest in marrying her. For Agnes, however, their consideration and desires could not compare to the Spouse that she had chosen, for she had consecrated her virginity to God. In this and in other aspects of her martyrdom, her story closely follows that of St. Lucy. One might conclude that perhaps their stories were conflated with each other, but it is also entirely possible that both suffered in much the same way, as human evil has its own limitations of creativity. Regardless, we will draw from the traditional stories of St. Agnes to present a full picture of piety and courage, for as the Catholic Encyclopedia notes, there is no "accurate and reliable narrative…on one point is there mutual agreement, viz., the youth of the Christian heroine." [3]

Despite a lack of agreement in the accounts, Agnes did have one important privilege. While many of her contemporary martyrs had their histories written by authors long forgotten (or purposefully anonymous), Agnes had some of the greatest orators and writers proclaim her story. Instead of arranging these martyrologies into a narrative, I will present a brief sketch of her martyrdom and then allow two of the original authors to tell their versions.

As mentioned before, Agnes had many young men interested in her. Of the numerous suitors who came calling and were turned away, at least one was frustrated enough to report her to the authorities as a

[3] Kirsch, Johann Peter, "St. Agnes of Rome", *The Catholic Encyclopedia*, Vol. 1 (New York: Robert Appleton Company, 1907). http://www.newadvent.org/cathen/01214a.htm

Madonna and Child with Saint Martina and Saint Agnes (detail)
El Greco, between 1597 and 1599
National Gallery of Art, Washington DC

Christian. This set in motion the ruthless and terribly efficient wheels of Roman justice. The accounts differ in what happened after Agnes's arrest. Some say that soldiers dragged her naked to a brothel, but her hair flowed over her body to preserve her modesty. Others state that she was condemned to burn to death, but the flames would not touch her. Most conclude with her death by the sword.

St. Ambrose, one of the most influential Church Fathers, was bishop of Milan in the 4th century. His love and wisdom helped convert St. Augustine of Hippo to the Faith, and he was a marvelous writer of both books and hymns. In fact, he is traditionally accredited with writing the incomparable *Te Deum* for the occasion of St. Augustine's baptism. One of his hymns is on the martyrdom of St. Agnes:

> *It is the blessed Virgin Agnes' feast, for today she was sanctified by shedding her innocent blood,*
> *and gave to heaven her heaven-claimed spirit.*
>
> *She that was too young to be a bride was old enough to be a martyr,*
> *and that too in an age when men were faltering in faith,*
> *and even hoary heads grew wearied and denied our God.*
>
> *Her parents trembled for their Agnes, and doubly did they thus defend the treasure of her purity; but her faith disdained a silent hiding-place, and unlocked its shelter-giving gate.*
>
> *One would think it was a bride hurrying with glad smiles*
> *to give some new present to her Spouse; and so it was:*
> *she was bearing to him the dowry of her martyrdom.*
>
> *They would fain make her light a torch at the altar*
> *of some vile deity they came to: "The Virgins of Jesus," said Agnes,*
> *"are not wont to hold a torch like this."*

"Its fire would quench one's faith; its flame would put out my light.
Strike, strike me, and the stream of my blood
shall extinguish these fires."

They strike her to the ground, and as she falls,
she gathers her robes around her, dreading, in the jealous purity of her
soul, the insulting gaze of some lewd eye.

Alive to purity even in the act of death, she buries her face in her
hands; and kneeling on the ground, she falls
as purity would wish to fall.

Glory be to thee, O Lord! and glory to thine Only Begotten Son,
together with thy Holy Spirit, for everlasting ages.[4]

The second account was written by Prudentius, a Christian poet of the 4th century. He visited Rome and witnessed its great devotion to St. Agnes. Inspired, he then wrote the following hymn/poem:

The tomb of Agnes, the intrepid maiden, the glorious Martyr,
is in the City of Romulus.
In her resting place, fronting the ramparts,
the Virgin watches over the sons of Quirinus;
and to pilgrims, too, that pray to her
with pure and faithful hearts,
she extends her protection.

She is a Martyr, that wears a double crown;
for she was a spotless, innocent virgin;

[4] Abbot Gueranger, *The Liturgical Year - Christmas*, tr. by Dom Laurence Shepherd (Dublin, James Duffy and Sons, 1886), 374-376.

Saint Agnes
Francesco Guarino, 1650
From an unknown collection

and a glorious victim that freely died for Christ.
It is related, that when a girl, and too young to be a bride,
she loved Jesus with tenderest love, and bravely withstood
the impious commands, that bade her offer sacrifice to the idols,
and deny the holy faith.

No art was left untried to make her yield:
the judge put on the softness of winning words,
and the grim executioner blustered out his threats—but Agnes stood
firm in stern courageousness, bidding them put her body
to their fierce tortures, for that she was willing to die.

Then spoke the fierce tyrant, "I know thy readiness
to suffer pain and tortures, and at how low a price
thou settest life; but there is one thing thou holdest dear—
a virgin's purity.
Tis this I have resolved to expose to insult in the common brothel,
unless thy head shall bend before the altar
of our virgin-goddess Minerva, and thou, a virgin that darest
to despise a virgin such as she, shalt humbly crave her pardon.
There shall youthful wantons have access,
and thou be minister to passion."

"And thinkest thou," said Agnes,
"that Christ can so forget his children, as to let our gold of purity
be robbed, and us be outcasts to his care?
He is ever with the chaste, shielding from injury
the gift he has bestowed of holy virginity.
Thy sword may drip, if so thou listest, with our blood;
but, contamination and dishonour, never!"

Scarce had she said these words, then order was given
to expose her in the vaults of the well-known street.
A throng, indeed, was there; but pity put a veil o'er every eye,
and fear imposed respect.
Save one alone, and gaze, he says, he will.
He scorns this modest fear, which checks the froward eye.
But lo! an Angel, swift as lightning, strikes and blinds
the wanton wretch. He falls, and writhes amidst the dust.
His fellows raise him from the ground, lifeless, as he seems to them;
and, weeping and lamenting, bear the corpse away.

Agnes had triumphed: and in a hymn of praise, she sings
her thanks to God the Father and his Christ, for that they had turned
the den of infamy into a shelter for her treasure,
and made virginity victorious.

Some say, that she was prayed to pray to Christ, that he would restore
the prostrate sinner to the vision he had lost:
she did so, and the youth regained his consciousness and sight.

But this was only one advance in heaven for our Saint;
a second is to come.
The cruel tyrant boils with furious wrath, and choked
with disappointment, exclaims: "Shall I be baffled by a girl?
Draw thy sword, soldier, and do the royal biddings
of our sovereign lord."

Agnes looked up, and saw the savage minion standing
with his unsheathed sword, and thus she spoke with beaming face:
"Oh! happy, happy change! A wild, fierce, boisterous swordsman,
for that young love-sick, smooth-faced, soft perfumed murderer
of the chaste soul!"

4th-century tomb roundel of St. Agnes (Via Saleria, Italy)

4th-century relief of St. Agnes from the altar at her tomb
The altar was originally built by Pope Liberius (352-366). The relief is now located at Sant'Agnese fuori le Mura in Rome.

*"This is a suitor that does please me. I will not run from him,
nor deny him what he asks. His steel shall nestle in my bosom,
and his sword shall warm in my heart's best blood.
Thus wedded to my Christ, I shall mount above this dark world
to the realms beyond the clouds.*

*"Eternal King! the gate of heaven, closed to men before thy coming
on our earth, is opened now—ah!
let me enter in.
Call to thyself, my Jesus, a soul that seeks but thee:
thy virgin-spouse, and thy Father's martyr—call me, Lord, to thee."*

*Thus did she pray; and then, with bended head, adored her Lord,
and in this posture was the readier to receive the uplifted sword.
The soldier's hand was raised,
and all the hopes of Agnes were fulfilled,
for with a single blow he beheads the holy maiden,
and death comes speedily to leave no time for pain.*

*Quickly her spirit quits its garb of flesh, and speeds untrammeled
through the air, surrounded, as it mounts,
by a choir of lovely Angels.*

*She sees this orb of ours far, far below, and all beneath her
seems a speck of dark. All earthly things are now so dwindled
to her spirit's eye, that she looks at them and smiles:—
yea, all seems poor:
the space traversed by the Sun,—the globe with all its system,—
all that lives in the stormy whirlwind of creation,
and changes with the vain fickleness of the world.*

*Kings and tyrants, empires and grades,
and the pompous pageantry of honours*

Saint Agnes

Master of the Bartholomew Altarpiece, latter half of 15th century

Alte Pinakothek, Munich

big with folly—the sovereignty of gold and silver,
which all men seek with rapid thirst, and gain by varied crime—
sumptuous dwellings—rich coloured garbs, mere graceful lies—
wrath and fear, hope and peril—grief so long, and joy so brief—
black envy's smoky flames, which blight men's hopes and fame—
and last but worst of all earth's ills,
the gloomy cloud of pagan superstition.

Agnes sees all this, and tramples on them all.
She stands, and crushes with her foot the serpent's head.
This monster, with his venom, taints all things on earth,
and plunges into hell the fools that are his slaves;
but, now, he crouching lies beneath a virgin's foot,
droops his fiery crest, and dares not raise his vanquished head.

And now, our God girds with two crowns the Virgin-Martyr's brow:
one is a sixtyfold of light eternal and reward:
the other is the hundredfold of fruit.

O happy Virgin! Singular in thy glory!
Noble inhabitant of heaven!
Decked with a twofold crown! Oh!
Look upon us who live in misery and sin; for, to thee alone
did our Heavenly Father give the power to change
impurity's abode into the shelter of chastity.

Fill my heart with the bright ray of thine intercession,
and I shall be cleansed; for all is pure, that can from thy pity
gain a look or loving visit.[5]

[5] Ibid., 376-382.

Her remains chiefly lie in two separate Roman churches. Her small, fragile skull is enshrined with honor in a chapel of Sant'Agnese in Agone in the Piazza Navona. It is also the location of the Circus Agonalis, and traditionally the site of the brothel where she was to be imprisoned. Her skull appears quite small, but perhaps its size reinforces the claim of its genuineness. For, if someone were choosing a head to display as a fraudulent relic of Agnes, they would pick one of average size for a girl her age, not one whose size would raise questions.

Her body lies in Sant'Agnese Fuori le Mura (St. Agnes Outside the Walls), which was built atop the Catacomb of St. Agnes. It is appropriate that two lambs are blessed by the Pope in this church on her feast day, for her Latin name is similar to that of agnus, or “lamb.” These lambs provide the wool that is woven into the pallia that are presented to new archbishops.

Saint Agnes, *pray for us.*

CECILIA

Martyred *in 230 A.D. in Rome*

Feast Day—*November 22nd*

But bright Cecilia raised the wonder high'r:
When to her organ, vocal breath was giv'n,
An angel heard, and straight appear'd,
Mistaking earth for Heav'n

Handel/Newburgh Hamilton, *Ode for St. Cecily*

In the Introduction, I mentioned that St. Cecilia had a strong influence in guiding this work. I decided to write her chapter last, even though she comes before St. Anastasia in the Roman Canon. One morning, with a few hours free, I decided it was time to start working on St. Cecilia's chapter, so I brought Bertha Lovewell's *The Life of St. Cecilia* to a local café and began reading. As I checked the date, I was amused to see it was November 22nd—the feast day of St. Cecilia.

THE STRUGGLE BEGINS

It was the middle of the night in the middle of the 9th century, and Archbishop Odo was bent over his desk, his eyes red-rimmed and

Saint Cecilia

Guido Reni, 1606

Norton Simon Museum, Pasadena

fatigued by the long hours of candlelight. While the rest of Vienna slept or crept about in the dark, he carefully transcribed and expanded the accounts from a dusty and decaying book named the *Parvum Romanum*. He had the good fortune to have discovered this ancient martyrology, and was adding its contents to the calendar of saints that he was writing. A deep sigh escaped his lips as he dipped into the inkpot and wrote:

> *On the X Kal. December. Cecilia, the blessed virgin, was born at Rome. She converted her husband Valerian and her brother Tiburtius to the faith, for which they endured martyrdom. Urban the Pope, moreover, as the result of her preaching, baptized no less than four hundred souls, among whom there was an illustrious man named Gordian.*
>
> *Thereupon Almachius commanded that the blessed Cecilia be brought to him, and when she held true to the faith, he commanded further that she be conducted to her own home and burned to death in its bath.*
>
> *Cecilia remained therein an entire day and night without injury, as if it had been a cold place. Hearing which, Almachius sent messengers who should behead her. These struck three blows but were not able to strike off her head. She lived after that for three days. Then St Urban, bearing away her body by night, buried it with the bodies of the popes. This blessed virgin lived during the times of the emperors Marcus Aurelius and Commodus.*
>
> *On the XVIII Kal. Maii. In Rome, via Appia, in the cemetery of Praetextatus, the holy martyrs Tiburtius, Valerian, and Maximus, under the prefect Almachius, slain by the sword (the last beaten with leaden plumbets until he gave up the ghost.)*

> *On the VIII Kal. Junii. In Rome, via Numentana, in the cemetery of Praetextatus, St. Urban, bishop and martyr, by whose teaching, in the time of the persecution of Alexander, many martyrs were crowned.*[1]

The archbishop read over his account and, while satisfied that it was an accurate summary of the works before him, nevertheless saw its poverty. Calendars of martyrs' feast days were terse and dry, like an account of a great battle in some centuries-old Greek history sitting on his bookshelf. They stated the facts, but they left one wanting more. "5,000 dead covered the battlefield" recorded part of a great struggle, but all the details of terror, courage, cowardice, and hatred hid in the depths behind a mere number, never to be known.

He quickly thumbed through his handwritten sheets, letting the calendar's dates and names of the dead flicker past in the pool of yellow light. As he stopped at St. Cecilia's entry, he thought of the incredible story he had heard about Pope Paschal [2] of blessed memory. Several decades ago, the Pope had found St. Cecilia's tomb in a catacomb, and her body was as intact and fresh as the moment she died. "Limitless are the wonders of God," the Archbishop muttered, and he smiled and went back to his work.

[1] Lovewell, Bertha Allen, *The Life of St. Cecilia* (Boston: Lamson, Wolffe, and Company, 1898), 16-17.

[2] Pope Pascal I. The second Pope Paschal would not reign until the 11th century, so Archbishop Odo would have simply known him as "Pope Paschal."

An old Italian postcard depicts the crypt of St. Cecilia within the Catacomb of St. Callixtus. The statue (a copy of the one created by Stefano Maderno) rests where her body was found.

THE POPE

Pope Paschal had a problem. In 821, he was praying in the Basilica of St. Cecilia in the Roman neighborhood of Trastevere, for he had a tender devotion to her. As he looked up from his meditations, he saw the woeful state of the august and ancient church. He had since worked to restore it and save it from falling into ruin, but he had failed to locate her relics. The Pope wanted St. Cecilia to rest in the church that bore her name, that others might pay their respects and be near her. According to tradition, she was buried near the Crypt of the Popes in the Catacomb of St. Callixtus on the Appian Way, but whether she was still hidden there or long removed, he did not know.[3] He put on his cloak against the rain and decided to try locating her again—alone this time.

He had visited the Crypt of the Popes many times since his own election in 817, descending the 4th-century stairway to its silent, cool depths to beg the prayers of those holy men. The catacomb itself ranged over five levels where half a million bodies rested in the nooks of the walls until Judgment Day, but it, too, was decaying and neglected. As he walked along the Appian Way, his hooded face shadowed, only one man bothered to set down his skin of wine and ask if this cloaked pilgrim wanted a tour of the catacombs. It was a bad sign to see only one of these tour guides about, for Rome used to be full of them. Pilgrims used to flood the Appian Way to visit the tombs and pay their respects, and the guides not only showed them the graves but kept them from getting lost in the black miles of passages. The Pope refused the offer but silently blessed the man. He would give him a few coins on his way back, but for now, he wanted to be anonymous.

With lamp lit, he descended the stairway into the Papal Crypt. It always galled him to see the devastation the Lombards had left in their wake after ransacking the catacombs in the 6th century—many of the tombs were broken, their epitaphs shattered and their contents long missing. After that invasion, the Popes had carefully removed as many of the illustrious remains as possible to protect them from future violence. Some said that the Lombards stole St. Cecilia's body, while others claimed to have her relics in their possession. The Pope was unconvinced by either possibility, and continued down the stairs.

[3] Abbot Gueranger, *Life of St. Cecilia* (Philadelphia: Peter F. Cunningham, 1866), 203.

Pulling off his cloak in the humid subterranean tomb, he crossed himself and held up the lamp to read the inscription posted in the Crypt of the Popes by Pope Damasus in the 4th century:

Here lies gathered, if you seek it, a host of holy people.
The venerated tombs hold the bodies of the saints,
The court of heaven has taken their sublime souls to itself.
Here are the companions of Sixtus, who bore off the trophy from the enemy;
Here is a group of Popes who guard the altars of Christ;
Here lies the bishop who lived long in peace;
Here are the holy confessors that Greece sent;
Here are the youths and children, old men and their chaste grandchildren
Who preferred to keep their virginal purity.
Here I, Damasus, confess I would have liked to be buried
But that I feared to vex the holy ashes of the saints.[4]

His gaze traveled over the walls near the Crypt of the Popes as his lips moved in a silent plea that Cecilia might reveal herself. A soft gleam from his lamp reflected off a wall tomb covered with a plain marble front, and it gently drew his attention. As he ran his fingers over its unbroken surface, the scent of lilies and roses perfumed the air, and he heard a young woman's voice, speaking with a marvelous freshness and gravity, say, "We owe thee many thanks! Take away my body, together with those of the other Saints near me, and place us in the Church thou hast recently restored." [5] He kissed the tomb with great joy and tried to slow his hurrying steps as he rushed into the open air. As he went past the unemployed tour guide and pushed a handful of gold coins into his hands, Pope Paschal exclaimed, "I found her! She's still there!" The man looked with amazement at the coins and the

[4] http://rome-honours-groningen.co.nf/2012/catacombsCal.php
[5] Gueranger, 206-207.

fleeing, cloaked man and thought, "Enthusiasm runs away with another poor fool." He shrugged, grinned, and turned his steps to the nearest wine shop.

As the Pope walked home, the majestic and pure voice of St. Cecilia still fresh in his memory, he thought about the incredible story of her life and death. He had read the most popular version of her *Acta* and wondered just how much of it was true, and how much was pious accretion. She was born in the early 200s into a noble pagan family, and her parents seemed to turn an indulgent eye towards the new Christian religion of their daughter. She was also a friend of Pope Urban, who had the challenging task of guiding his flock in a time when persecution, though cooled by Emperor Alexander Severus's policies, still claimed its victims. The Pope may have even received Cecilia's vow to virginity, a pledge that led not only to her martyrdom but to the salvation of her companions.

Her trials began when her parents arranged a marriage with a wealthy pagan, Valerian. Cecilia met this challenge with prayer and penance, wearing a hair shirt under her garments and undertaking fasts of several days, begging God's help with unceasing petition. God seemed deaf to her pleas, for her wedding day arrived. She met her groom with her hair "divided into six tresses, which was at once an imitation of the Vestal headdress, and a touching symbol of Cecilia's consecration." [6] Some say that she sat apart during the wedding party and sang the praises of God to herself, making her the beloved patroness of musicians. That night, she confided her vow of virginity to her husband Valerian, who then ran to Pope Urban to be baptized and received into the Church. According to legend, an angel appeared and

[6] Ibid., 61.

crowned Cecilia and Valerian, who was now wearing the white garment of the baptized, with roses and lilies.[7] Pope Paschal chuckled to himself as he remembered this part of the story. It must have taken quite a woman (and perhaps a few powerful visions and miracles) to convince an ardent young man to forsake his honeymoon and take up the life of a celibate husband.

Valerian's conversion sparked the Holy Spirit into flame in the soul of his brother, Tiburtius, who also went to Pope Urban for baptism. They devoted themselves to gathering up the remains of those Christians who were sentenced to death by a particularly savage prefect named Almachius. Emperor Alexander Severus was campaigning far from Rome, so Almachius felt free to exercise a bit of his loathing towards these disobedient Christians who refused to sacrifice to the gods that kept the empire safe. Tiburtius and Valerian would visit the sites of the executions and carefully collect the battered remains, soaking up the blood with sponges and pouring it into sealed ampullae that they interred with the bodies.

The two brothers soon fell under the searching gaze of Almachius, and he sentenced them to death by beheading when they refused to offer incense to idols. The soldier who accompanied them, named Maximus, was so impressed by their witness that he declared his conversion to the Faith. For this betrayal, Almachius had Maximus beaten to death with whips tipped with leaden balls. Cecilia suffered all of this with joy and abandonment to God's will, and took care of burying their remains and preparing herself for a similar fate.

Almachius had not forgotten about Cecilia, for he devised a means of killing her that would not only be lengthy and painful, but hidden. He knew how beloved and popular she was within the Church, and he did not want to push his persecutions to the point of revolt, so he

[7] Ibid., 71.

determined to kill her quietly. Her family's wealth had provided Cecilia with the luxury of a private caldarium, or steam room. He would order her locked in the room, and the fire stoked until she was suffocated by its tremendous heat. Cecilia happily entered this place of combat and was still alive after an entire day and night, seemingly untouched by the steam. An exasperated Almachius ordered her head cut off, but the trembling executioner, perhaps intimidated by her presence and courage, failed to kill her after three brutal strokes. According to the law, he could strike no more, and he fled the room.

Cecilia lay on the floor, the blood pooling from her neck. The faithful arrived and crowded around her, stanching the blood with linen cloths. For three days she suffered and urged them to be faithful, and she ordered her remaining wealth to be distributed to the poor. Finally, she called for Pope Urban, and he knelt beside his tormented, yet smiling, daughter. She said, "I asked this delay of three days, from our Lord, that I might place in the hands of your Beatitude, my last treasure, the poor whom I feed and who will miss me. I also bequeath to you this house in which I have lived, that you may consecrate it as a church, and that it may become the temple of the Lord forever." This said, she turned on her side and died.[8]

[8] Ibid., 129.

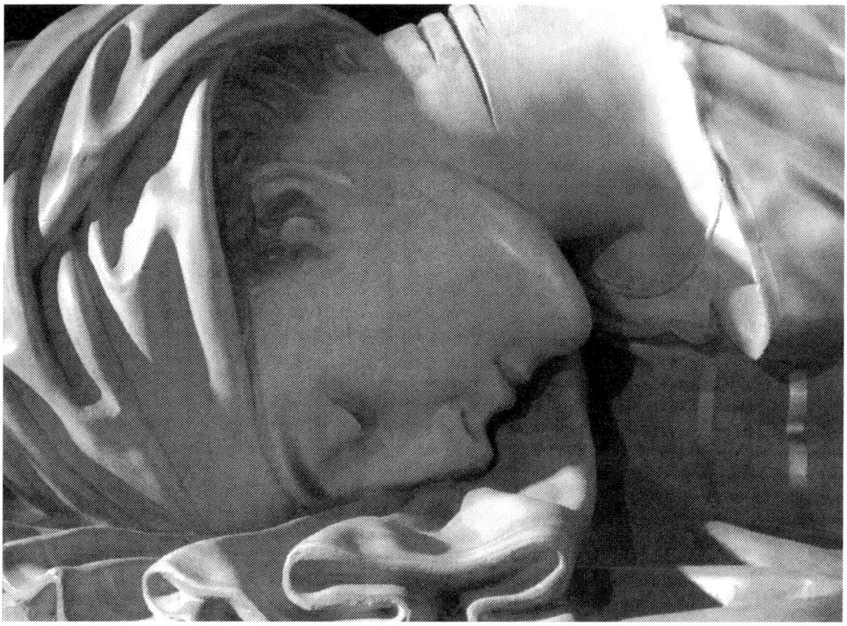

Painted replica of Stefano Maderno's statue of St. Cecilia (detail)[9]
St. Cecilia Cathedral, Albi, France

Still musing on this story, Pope Paschal reached his palace and quickly assembled his most trusted team of excavators and historians, and, though night was coming, they hurried back to the catacombs. The workers carefully chipped away at the mortar around the marble covering until all was ready. Holding his breath, the Pope watched as they removed the slab. At once, the scent of lilies and roses again permeated the air, mixed with the deep notes of myrhh, as if an unseen angel was swinging a censor and blessing the cypress coffin that was revealed to their sight.

They lowered her coffin to the ground and delicately pried off the top. Inside lay a small young woman. She rested on her right side, her

[9] Photo by Mamjodh (CC Attribution 2.0 Generic License).

head veiled, her body clothed in a silken garment fringed with gold. Her legs were drawn up in a semi-fetal position within the small confines of the coffin. At her bare feet lay the blood-stained linen cloths that had soaked up her blood. Pope Paschal touched her feet with a trembling hand, and, though cool, they were supple, utterly untouched by decay. It was as if she had entered the tomb that very day.

Nearby they discovered the bones of Valerian, Tiburtius, and Maximus. All four martyrs were processed in triumph and interred in St. Cecilia's church with great pomp. Pope Paschal was careful to leave St. Cecilia's incorrupt body within its cypress coffin, precisely as he found her, only adding a beautiful damask lining and veiling her body with silk. He ordered the remains of her beloved Pope Urban interred with the martyrs, and there they rested for the next eight centuries.

THE CARDINAL

In 1599, Cardinal Sfondrato had a problem. He was the titulary of St. Cecilia's, and had restored much of the church; and yet, he had failed to locate the burial place of St. Cecilia and her companions. Over the years, he had collected an extensive collection of relics and wanted to place them with the revered saint. He knew Pope Paschal I had buried her somewhere under the altar, a practice mirroring Revelation 6:9—"And when he broke the fifth seal, I saw there, beneath the altar, the souls of all who had been slain for love of God's word and of the truth they held." The best course of action, he decided, was to tear up the floor and see what was beneath.

St. Cecilia's *confessio*. This subterranean crypt beneath St. Cecilia's in Rome allows direct access with her relics that lie beneath the altar. The small altar to the left faces her tomb.[10]

[10] Photo by Claudiu Georgescu (CC Attribution ShareAlike 3.0 License).

As the workers cracked through the foundations beneath the altar, they opened up a chamber that contained two white marble sarcophagi. The Cardinal quickly ordered witnesses and chroniclers to come and document the discovery, and he anxiously paced until they arrived. When all was ready, the tombs were opened. Once again, the cypress coffin came to light.

The damask lining had faded a bit, but Cecilia was still unmarred by time. Inside the other sarcophagus, they found the remains of Valerian, Tiburtius, and Maximus. One body was missing its head: this was Tiburtius, whose skull was known to be in a separate reliquary within the church. Another set of remains had a skull that was shattered and fractured: this was Maximus, whom the *Acta* declared was beaten to death by loaded whips. The remaining skeleton was similar in size and age to Tiburtius: his brother Valerian.

All of Rome rejoiced as the martyrs' veiled remains were triumphantly displayed in the church for veneration. Cardinal Sfondrato commissioned a young sculptor, Stefano Maderno, to memorialize St. Cecilia in stone. Stefano, only 24 years old, captured her incorrupt body with exquisite beauty and precision. He portrayed her as she lay in her coffin, for the Cardinal forbade any moving of her body. The sculpture shows that her head is turned at an unnatural angle, most likely due to the vicious sword blows that nearly severed her neck, and her face is veiled and turned away from the viewer. Her right hand has three fingers extended to represent the Trinity, while her left hand extends a single finger signifying that God is one.

Saint Cecilia
Stefano Maderno, 1600
Church of St. Cecilia, Rome [11]

Over 400 years have passed since Cecilia and her companions were once again sealed within their tombs beneath the altar. Empires have risen and collapsed, Rome has suffered under Fascists and Nazis, and untold millions have come to see the white marble figure before the altar. Displayed against an inky black backdrop, the sculpture anticipates the Baroque period of dramatic light and shadow, as if Cecilia is once again witnessing to her faith on a stage before her accusers. Her wounds proclaim her fidelity to her Lord, and one can almost catch a hint of lilies and roses that waft from the sleeping figure wrapped in silk that rests in silence until the final trumpet sounds.

[11] Photo by Richard Stracke (CC Attribution 1.0 Generic license).

So when the last and dreadful hour
This crumbling pageant shall devour,
The trumpet shall be heard on high,
The dead shall live, the living die,
And music shall untune the sky.

Handel/Newburgh Hamilton, *Ode to St. Cecily*

Saint Cecilia, *pray for us.*

The Ecstasy of Saint Cecilia
Raphael, 1514
Pinacoteca Nazionale, Bologna

ANASTASIA

Martyred *in 304 A.D. in Sirmium (modern Serbia)*

Feast Day*—December 25th*

Why should I rail on fortune or repine?
Why should I grieve? God's remedy is mine.
Endure then, as philosophers maintain
A brave man should, adversity and pain.

Blessed Thomas Belson[1]

The last saint invoked in the Canon, Anastasia, is perhaps the least known of the seven in the Western Church. Perpetua and Felicity have a rich and authentic *Passio* and archaeological fame. Lucy appears throughout Dante's *Divine Comedy* and has the memorable iconography of her eyes resting on a platter. Agnes and Agatha are firmly rooted in western piety and art, while Cecilia's patronage of musicians has ensured a place for her image and intercession in choir lofts worldwide. For Anastasia, one of the most treasured female saints of the early Church, the centuries have brought greater obscurity.

One reason for this might be the confusion over her identity. According to the scholar Jane Baun, there are three distinct St. Anastasias with different feast days, but their stories and hagiographies

[1] Martyred in England in 1589 for assisting priests, he most likely wrote these lines while imprisoned in the Tower of London.

Saint Anastasia

Late 14th century

State Hermitage Museum, St. Petersburg

have intertwined and overlapped over the centuries.[1] As the *Catholic Encyclopedia* of 1911 succinctly states, "All that is certain is that a martyr named Anastasia gave her life for the faith in Sirmium, and that her memory was kept sacred in that church." [2] Since we are approaching St. Anastasia from a posture of devotion, we will ask her to enlighten our souls despite the confusion of the narratives, that she might assist us in these confusing times.

On the Palatine Hill in Rome there is a church, still in use, that the Catholic community built in the 4th century after the persecutions had ended—Santa Anastasia al Palatino. At the time, it was among the most important churches in the city, and one of the original 25 *tituli*, or parish, churches of Rome. Inside, the early Christians reverently stored the crosses that they held aloft during the processions to different "stational" churches in the city. These processions were (and are—they are still held to this day) incredibly ancient practices that formed out of the early Church's tradition of visiting the martyrs' tombs as a group and then celebrating the Mass.[3] The name "station" (in Latin, a "watch" or "standing position") may have been applied to these gatherings and processions because of their penitential nature. As St. Ambrose of the 4th century wrote, "Our fasts are our encampments against the attacks of the devil; they are called *stationes* because we remain standing." Thus, each station church "became the place before which or within which the faithful walked in procession and, tired out, but always

[1] Baun, Jane, *Tales from Another Byzantium: Celestial Journey and Local Community in the Medieval Greek Apocrypha* (Cambridge: Cambridge University Press, 2007), 117-120.
[2] Kirsch, Johann Peter, "St. Anastasia", *The Catholic Encyclopedia*, Vol. 1 (New York: Robert Appleton Company, 1907).
http://www.newadvent.org/cathen/01453a.htm
[3] Phillip Barrows Whitehead, "The Church of S. Anastasia in Rome," *American Journal of Archaeology* 31, no. 4 (Oct. - Dec. 1927): 405.

St. Anatasia between St. Roch (l) and St. Thomas of Canterbury (r)

Late 15th century

Cappella di Sant'Anastasia in Sale San Giovanni, Piedmont

standing [*statio*], sometimes leaning on a stick, assisted, before separating, at the celebration of the Liturgy." [4]

St. Anastasia's on the Palatine not only held the distinction of displaying the processional crosses, but was one of the most revered of the station churches. Built in the center of ancient Rome, St. Anastasia was one of the three churches where the Pope celebrated the Mass on December 25th, the others being St. Peter's and Santa Maria Maggiore. This was due to December 25th formerly being associated with the feast of St. Anastasia before Christmas was established on the same date.

Thus, one of Rome's most beloved saints drew back her prominence to make room for her Savior. This decrease in her popularity continued throughout the centuries until today, when it is the rarest visitor to Rome who has St. Anastasia's on the Palatine on his tour itinerary.

This church is also important because it may hold the key to explain why there are so many tangled threads in St. Anastasia's story. Let us interweave more of its history with the legends associated with Anastasia so that, God willing, it creates a beautiful tapestry in her honor.

To begin, it is uncertain which Anastasia the early community had in mind when they built the church. For if St. Anastasia was martyred in Sirmium in the early 300s, it is nearly impossible that her *cultus* would have spread to Rome quickly enough to inspire not only a church in her name, but one of the most important churches in the city. More likely, there are two possible explanations for its name. St. Anastasia's was recorded in very early documents as a titular, or "titled", church, which meant that its name came from that of a donor or provider (in

[4] Leclercq, Henri, "Station Days", *The Catholic Encyclopedia*, Vol. 14. (New York: Robert Appleton Company,1912).
http://www.newadvent.org/cathen/14268a.htm

some cases, the donor was unwilling, as in the Lateran Basilica, named after the Lateranus family whose land was seized by Constantine.) Thus, there may have been a wealthy Roman donor named Anastasia who provided the means to build the church.

Another possibility is that the word *anastasis* in Greek refers to the Resurrection of Christ, and churches of that name were established in other parts of the Empire. The Greek word *anastasis* thus developed into a "St. Anastasia", and the legends accrued and attached over time.

One of these "Anastasia histories" from the medieval *Golden Legend* is that there was a young Roman woman named Anastasia whose father was called Praetextatus. He was a *vir illustris*, one of the most important men in Rome, perhaps a senator.[5] Her mother was a Christian who learned the Faith from St. Chrysogonus, himself a martyr who also had a church dedicated to him in Rome. Against Anastasia's wishes, her father forced a marriage to a pagan man named Publius, but Anastasia kept her virginity through a steadfast feigning of illness. She would secretly go about the city and do good deeds for others, visiting Christian prisoners and distributing her husband's wealth to the poor. He soon caught on to her activities, and kept her locked in her room, intending to starve her to death. Instead, her husband died and she was set free.

Three Christian sisters then moved in with Anastasia, but they soon drew the lustful attention of a local official. One day, he burst into the kitchen to rape them as his gang waited outside to watch the entrances to the home. The three fell to their knees in prayer and the official suddenly became deranged, grasping and kissing the sooty pots and pans until he was covered with grime. He fled from the home only to have his companions leave him in disgrace. After various other humiliating episodes, he was able to arrange the execution of the three

[5] "St. Anastasia", *Catholic Encyclopedia*.

virgin sisters and punished Anastasia through another forced marriage to a pagan. Eventually, her refusals of sacrifice to the pagan gods (and her refusal to share her bed with her husband) gained her exile and martyrdom through burning. The *Golden Legend* concludes that "Apollonia, which was a Christian woman, toke the body of S. Anastasia, and buried it in her garden, and there did do make a fair church."[6]

While these accounts are quite fantastic and have no historical basis, it is interesting to see their ties with the church of St. Anastasia. Many of the more legendary lives of the saints are generated over centuries by combining places and stories into a cohesive whole. Did these early narrators have her Roman church in mind when they spoke of the "fair church" that arose over her grave? Perhaps they wove another established church's namesake, St. Chrysogonus, into the story to give it further weight and authority. Other variations of the story have her exiled to the island of Palmaria, and there beheaded. Of course, there may have truly been a martyr whose life is the basis of these colorful accounts, but the intervening centuries have swallowed up anything certain.

More likely, St. Anastasia suffered martyrdom in Sirmium just before the persecutions ended in the early 300s. Since Sirmium is near the eastern borders of the empire, her *cultus* made its way to the newly founded capital of the East, Constantinople, by the mid-400s. In the East, she became known as St. Anastasia the Pharmakolitria—the Deliverer from Potions. Icons show Anastasia holding a vial in one of her hands and a cross in the other, for she is revered as both an exorcist and a healer from spells, potions, and poisons. As officials traveled

[6] De Voragine, Jacobus, *The Golden Legend (as Englished by William Caxton, Volume II)*, edited by F.S. Ellis (London: J.M. Dent and Co., 1900), 151.

St. Anastasia with Elijah (far left) and St. Nicholas of Myra

Early 15th century

State Tretyakov Gallery, Moscow

between Constantinople and Rome, they brought their devotion to St. Anastasia the Pharmakolitria with them. Since the church of Anastasia was located near the center of the political and official life of Rome, it was a natural step to associate it with this newly arrived Eastern martyr. By the end of the 5th century, she was so famous that her name was added to the Roman Canon.

As noted before, the years brought decline and a fading of her memory, and her church that once stood in the center of Roman life now has a more humble station. As the *Catholic Encyclopedia* notes with a tinge of sadness, "this ancient sanctuary stands today quite isolated amid the ruins of Rome. The commemoration of St. Anastasia in the second Mass on Christmas day is the last remnant of the former prominence enjoyed by this saint and her church in the life of Christian Rome." Perhaps we who now have a greater understanding of St. Anastasia—both the church and the martyr—might take a moment to ask her intercession in our lives, and make the effort to visit the sanctuary that bears her name should we find ourselves in the Eternal City.

Saint Anastasia, *pray for us.*

While walking the Camino Portuguese in 2019, I took refuge from the rain under a portico of a little church dedicated to the female martyr St. Marina. Saint Marina, *pray for us*.

Matthew Manint resides in Biloxi, Mississippi. He is a consecrated man who follows the spirituality of Blessed Charles de Foucauld. Bl. Charles's inspirations were the hidden life of Jesus at Nazareth and being a brother to all.

Printed in Great Britain
by Amazon

48180473R00078